Praise for *The Encore Curve*

"With the right mind-set and planning, anyone can have a future that becomes increasingly more fascinating and motivating regardless of age. In this book, Andy Raub shows how creatively rethinking purpose and money can make retirement into an opportunity to build an exceptional life of growth and opportunity you'll look forward to waking up to every day."

—Dan Sullivan, founder of The Strategic Coach, Inc.

"I am glad that there are people like Andy in the world who are bringing peace, abundance, and meaning into our lives. Andy is America's Encore Coach!"

—Jack Canfield, America's number-one success coach and cocreator of the Chicken Soup for the Soul series

"*The Encore Curve* teaches us how to make our retirement encore better than our main performance. Having a plan ready that saves our best for last should excite us all. Here's to the encore!"

—Colleen Bowler, CFP®, author of *Generous Kids*

"Having written and spoken about relationships for years, I know how major life transitions like retirement can stress our bonds with others. *The Encore Curve* provides practical tools for navigating this time with meaning, a clearer direction, more predictable results, and stronger relationships."

—Robert Hall, retired CEO of ActionSystems and author of *This Land of Strangers: The Relationship Crisis That Imperils Home, Work, Politics, and Faith*

"Andy Raub has the process, tools, and expertise to help you design a compelling future. If you're looking for clarity and a process for laying out your next chapter, *The Encore Curve* will energize and equip you to determine your true north."

—Daniel Allen, advisor to executive leaders and author
of *Summoned: Stepping Up to Live and Lead with Jesus*

"Andy Raub has penned a wise and engaging challenge to those of us facing retirement. *The Encore Curve* delivers on its promise to provide a reinvigorating life plan and a money plan that will calm your fears."

—Dr. Reg Grant, chair and senior professor of media
arts and worship at Dallas Theological Seminary

"A great read if you are serious about taking charge of your life as you experience changes. The story carries you along, and the coaching instructions are easy to follow. This book can change the way you think about your future."

—Clyde C. Jackson Jr., chairman and
CEO of Wynne/Jackson, Inc.

"*The Encore Curve* uses faith, optimism, and humor to help you traverse the slippery slope of financial security. It teaches you how to grow old with confidence and peace. Great read."

—Suzie Humphreys, "independent woman,"
humorist, and inspirational speaker

"Retirement is a dream for many of us. But if you don't properly prepare for it, it can quickly turn into a nightmare. Andy Raub's book gives us the tools we need to retire with money, purpose, and pride. I love it!"

—Starlene Stringer, radio and TV personality
and best-selling author

THE
ENCORE
CURVE

THE
ENCORE
CURVE

Retire with a Life
Plan That Excites You

ANDY RAUB

BROWN BOOKS
PUBLISHING GROUP

The Encore Curve
Retire with a Life Plan That Excites You

Brown Books Publishing Group
16250 Knoll Trail Drive, Suite 205
Dallas, Texas 75248
www.BrownBooks.com
(972) 381-0009

A New Era in Publishing®

ISBN 978-1-61254-893-7
LCCN 2016954512

Printed in the United States
10 9 8 7 6 5 4 3 2 1

Publisher's Cataloging-In-Publication Data
Names: Raub, Andy.
Title: The Encore Curve : retire with a life plan that excites you / Andy Raub.
Description: Dallas, Texas : Brown Books Publishing Group, [2017] | Includes
    bibliographical references.
Identifiers: LCCN 2016954512 | ISBN 978-1-61254-893-7 | ISBN 978-1-61254-
    977-4 (ebook)
Subjects: LCSH: Finance, Personal. | Retirement income. | Retirement--Planning.
Classification: LCC HG179 .R38 2017 (print) | LCC HG179 (ebook) | DDC
    332.024/014--dc23

For more information or to contact the author, please go to
www.EncoreCurve.com.

To my wife, Jean:

You show me each day what Encore Curve living is all about—using your gifts and passions to impact the lives of those around you. Thanks for always inspiring me to be more than I can be by myself.

Contents

Acknowledgments

Even though my name is on the cover as author of this book, it is a product of the collective wisdom and hard work of a great team. Many of the ideas germinated from the genius of Dan Sullivan, my mentor for many years and the founder of Strategic Coach®. Thank you, Dan, for teaching me new ways to package my wisdom.

All of the inspiration in the world is useless without perspiration. Kelli Sallman, my editor and cowriter, took my ideas and turned them into something workable. She is a great writer and an even better teacher and friend. Kelli, thanks for pushing me further down the trail than I thought I could go and for keeping this project on track.

Kristi Cole, marketer extraordinaire, has been the perfect guide to deal with all the intricacies of graphic art, web design, and social media. We make a great team, and I really appreciate your patience in teaching this tech-challenged soul the same lessons repeatedly.

I am blessed with an extraordinary team in my day job at Raub Capital Management. Sarah Crowe, Kim Parker, and Lynne Thurston have worked hard to keep our business moving forward and serve our clients as I wandered into the world of authorship. Thanks for your friendship and loyalty.

Thanks to Milli Brown and the great team at Brown Books. Milli, you have changed the paradigm of book publishing and have pulled together an amazing group of people, to whom I'm indebted. Special thanks to Tom Reale and his team, who have guided the editing and publishing, and to Cathy Williams and her Agency at Brown Books colleagues, who are steering us along the rocky road of making a book successful.

In keeping with the spirit of "the first shall be last," my wife Jean has been my greatest inspiration for over forty-nine years. Jean is the epitome of someone who maximizes her encore. She spends countless hours serving others and making their lives better. She challenges me by asking the hard questions, and she encourages me to chase my own Encore Curve visions. Jean also shows me every day what it means to faithfully follow God's leading. Thank you for being my partner on this great roller-coaster ride we call life. I love you.

Introduction

I have never liked riding roller coasters. I prefer to stay in control and know where I'm going next. Unfortunately, my grandchildren love them. Several years ago, my wife, Jean, and I took our two daughters and their families to Disney World to celebrate our anniversary. The biggest and baddest roller coaster–type ride they could find was something called Expedition Everest. The whole family lined up to ride, but Jean and I stayed behind to guard all our stuff. After everyone had finished the ride, the conversation for the rest of the day was about how scary it had been: all the vertical climbs, the sudden drops in the dark, and especially the yeti monster that jumped out to frighten everyone.

The next day, my intrepid youngest grandson, Kyle, insisted on returning to the coaster and riding again. Kyle was six years old and couldn't convince any other adults to join him for the second go-round, so I volunteered. As we were standing in line awaiting our fate, Kyle, with his vast experience, went into great detail about what we were soon to encounter: the dark climbs, the gut-wrenching dives, and, of course, the leaping yeti creature. Finally, just before we were strapped into the car, Kyle looked up at me and said, "Dandy"—that's my grandpa name—"you're gonna scream like a little girl."

Guess what? I did.

Let me ask you a question. Does life ever make you scream? You know the feeling: thrilling triumphs followed by sudden falls in the dark. Then, just when you think things are back to normal, a monster jumps out and scares you to death. Changes happen to all of us, but sometimes it feels as though we've been strapped into a giant roller coaster with no control and no end in sight. Many of us feel as though we are balanced precariously between what was and what will be, and we're not sure what will happen next.

For more than thirty-five years, I have worked as a financial advisor and investment manager for families and retirees. During this time, I've had the privilege of helping hundreds of clients work their way through all kinds of transitions, such as retirement, serious illness, or the death of a loved one. Some transitions come about because we choose them, which allows us to build a plan and prepare. Other changes, however, seem to choose us and offer no alternative. Experience tells me we should all prepare for the certainty of uncertainty. But how can we do that?

> Many of us feel as though we are balanced precariously between what was and what will be, and we're not sure what will happen next.

I have noticed that most life transitions ultimately raise two types of questions. First there is a time question: "Now what am I going to do?" Then there is a money question: "Will I have enough money?" During retirement, these two questions imply unstated fears: "I'm afraid I will outlive my meaning or significance!" and "I'm afraid I will outlive my money or income!" Although this book focuses on retirement, I hope you will find it helpful for any roller-coaster life experiences you encounter.

Today's Retirement Is a Different Animal

For many of us, retirement is that looming life change that we're either preparing to face in the near future or have just entered. I know—I'm right there with you. I'm an early baby boomer, and I find myself thinking more and more about retirement. But the retirement I'm thinking of doesn't look like the experience my parents or your parents knew—it's a different animal altogether. One definition of retirement is "to be taken out of production." Most people my age, however, want to keep being productive well into their later years. They certainly don't want to be taken out of production.

The idea of retiring at a certain age originated during the Industrial Revolution. Back then, people traded their physical labor for a paycheck. The value of workers decreased as their physical energy and endurance waned with age. Consequently, employers readily replaced them with younger, stronger, and possibly cheaper workers. Today, our paychecks often come from our intellectual capital and experience rather than from our physical abilities. Instead of decreasing in value, these more intellectual attributes often become more valuable with age.

The system for forcing retirement at a particular age is attributed to Chancellor Otto von Bismarck of 1880s Germany. At that time, retirement was mandated at age seventy even though the average life expectancy for German workers was only forty-six. The idea took root in the United States during the Great Depression as a

3

way to move older workers out of the workforce and younger workers into it. During this period, the government created the Social Security system to help workers retire at age sixty-five. Even then, average life expectancy was only around sixty-two. No one really envisioned the financial or emotional cost of a longer life expectancy.

Today's retirees face several conflicting scenarios. First, life expectancy statistics imply that today's baby boomers could easily live another thirty years beyond retirement without a regular paycheck. Some could actually spend more time in retirement than they did in their working careers. Second, with the rising price of medical care and other costs, these years could be far more expensive than any of us imagine. Most retirees are poorly equipped, both emotionally and economically, to manage a dwindling amount of money in the face of increasing costs.

Yet if, as stated earlier, our intellectual capital increases as we age, why should we suddenly shut it down? Why should we stop using our experience and abilities to make an impact on the important things and people in our lives? According to a Pew Research survey, baby boomers believe old age begins sometime after age seventy-two, and typical boomers feel nine years younger than their actual ages.[1] While some continue to work past full retirement age, many of today's retirees now see retirement as a time for leisure with a purpose. Most—whether working or not—want to be significant and continue to make a difference well into their senior years. Most people, however, have never learned to restructure their finances and plan their lives to take advantage of these later-life opportunities and challenges.

This book is divided into two sections: "A Life Plan That Excites You" and "A Money Plan That Lets You Sleep." Each section helps you answer one of the two questions I mentioned earlier: "What am I going to do with the rest of my life?" and "Will I have enough money to live on?" These two questions are intertwined. You can't answer the money question without clearly defining the significance question, and you cannot solve the significance question until you have reached some conclusions about the money question. The answer to each question feeds the other.

Will I Outlive My Significance?

One of my favorite movies is the 1987 classic *The Princess Bride*. In this movie, actor Mandy Patinkin plays a character named Inigo Montoya whose whole life is dedicated to finding and killing the six-fingered man who murdered his father. Throughout the movie, he confronts people with this now-famous line: "Hello. My name is Inigo Montoya. You killed my father. Prepare to die."

At the end of the movie, however—after he has finally succeeded in finding and killing the murderer—he utters another unforgettable line that frames our retirement question: "You know, it is very strange. I have been in the revenge business so long. Now that it is over, I don't know what to do with the rest of my life."

Like Inigo, many of us just aren't yet ready to "pack it in" and adjust to life without working (or seeking revenge). The good news is that retirement is changing. It's being redefined by people just like you who are choosing to think in terms of the "next phase of life" rather than retirement in its traditional sense. This is a major paradigm shift that opens up all sorts of new and exciting possibilities. In fact, many people now view retirement at age sixty-five not so much as an artificial finish line but as a potential starting line.

This "next phase of life" thinking presents us with fresh chances to make several midcourse corrections, including the following:

- Recreating our life plans so they center on goals and values we lacked the time or freedom to pursue when we were working full time
- Achieving a balance between leisure time and satisfying pursuits that continue to shape us as people and that give back to others in meaningful ways
- Organizing our finances so we can tell our money where we want it to go rather than letting it drift away without proper supervision
- Building a contingency plan for sudden changes to our lives or health that might otherwise drain our resources and leave us in the danger zone

Essentially, "next phase" planning gives us a chance to refocus our lives by choosing to put first things first. We can be intentional about our pursuits and purposeful about where we spend our time. We can create our own plans rather than allow ourselves to be driven by the agendas and demands of others.

The first part of this book offers a coaching process that will give you the tools you need to define your own next phase. I call this strategy the Encore Curve because we all want to finish strong and give our world a memorable encore that presents the best of who we are. As we age, we tend to slowly decline. We lose energy, focus, and purpose. We run the risk of letting our past become bigger and more exciting than our future. I want to show you some ways to create and follow a powerful vision for your future, regardless of your age. We should retire *to* something compelling rather than *from* something we want to escape. Creating a big vision for your future is the first step.

Will I Outlive My Money?

This question is at the heart of every decision to retire. Obviously, it costs money to live. What happens when we stop earning money and must let the wealth we have accumulated provide our income? That, my friends, is perhaps the scariest transition we ever face. As with jumping out of an airplane without a parachute, we suddenly find ourselves flying free with no backup plan.

Think of your money life as if you were climbing a mountain. We spend most of our lives climbing up the mountain as we work to save and accumulate money. When we have a steady paycheck and lots of time, we have some room for error. We can be more aggressive, take some risks, and still have time to recover from mistakes. But seasoned mountain climbers will tell you that the most dangerous part of the climb is rounding the top and descending back down. That's when the journey changes. Decisions become more critical. Mistakes are compounded in the thin air and dangerous terrain. The rules of the retirement game change once you begin descending the mountain. The margin for error shrinks. You are no longer accumulating; you are spending. What if you run out of provisions halfway down? What if your journey takes longer than planned? What if your health fails and the journey becomes more difficult?

These are the money fears that plague most retirees, and they are well founded, since the descent lasts the rest of your life. In the second part of this book, we will look at techniques for managing your money on your way down the mountain. Don't expect fancy investment advice or secrets to beating the market. Those are not the tools we need as we descend. You *can* expect wisdom gained from years of being a mountain guide who has successfully helped hundreds of clients down the mountain. I call these techniques the

Peace of Mind Investor Process because they can help reduce your anxiety about money during retirement.

Write Your Own Story

I have written this book in the form of a story because each person's life is a story being written as he or she lives out every day. Each character in *The Encore Curve* is a fictional version of someone whom I have had the privilege of knowing. Throughout the book I offer tools and exercises that can help you design your own answers to these questions about life and money. To gain the greatest value from this book, complete all the exercises. Your answers may shift or change as you move through them. As you complete each exercise, feel free to go back and adjust or reevaluate prior exercises based on your new wisdom.

I hope you find the coaching process in this book to be one you can use on a continuing basis. At the ends of certain chapters, you will find small versions of worksheets that may be downloaded and printed from our website. To access the full set of worksheets, visit www.EncoreCurve.com/worksheets, where you will also find a complete suite of coaching tools to lead you through your discovery process.

I want to give you a final word of encouragement as you get strapped into your roller-coaster seat. You may think that having a fulfilling and worry-free retirement is reserved for someone else, not you. Not true. You may believe that finding a new and exciting way to finish strong is for someone who has already accomplished a lot. Not necessarily. You may feel as though living a life filled with a great amount of financial confidence is only for the wealthy. That's not true either. With the right tools, you can create the retirement of your dreams.

Regardless of where you find yourself as you face this great transition called "retirement," I hope this book will provide not only a word of encouragement but also a way to find your personal path to a life well finished. My prayer is that you will build your own encore performance at the end of your personal play—an encore in which you give it the best that you have and you leave your audience on its feet, cheering for more, as your curtain slowly descends. Now that's a great ride!

Thanks for reading, and enjoy your journey.

Andy Raub

A Life Plan That Excites You

1

The Future Is Closer Than You Think

"What can a man do who doesn't know what to do?"

—Milton Mayer, journalist

On a Monday morning, George Morris scrolled through his inbox, culling out all the junk. As he clicked on the next e-mail in the list, his hand froze. His foot stopped tapping. He read the electronic memo again:

This e-mail serves as notice that your department or position is being considered for reorganization. You will qualify for an early retirement package. We advise you to begin analyzing your financial situation to see if this option will benefit you.

George highlighted the words "early retirement." He straightened his stapler and the picture of his grandkids on his desk.

Retirement. George had worked for the same engineering firm for the past twenty-seven years. He liked the creative design part of his job and had built a comfortable niche within the company as a design expert in certain critical areas. In fact, he had left his first job with Mammoth, a much bigger company, for this smaller local company because they had recruited him to specialize in design engineering. That decision had proven to be one of his best. During the past year, however, his company had been sold and merged into Worldwide Engineering, a much larger, multinational company. Since the merger, the stress level at the office had risen; everyone was on edge and wondering what would happen. Now George began to see that his future plans were probably going to change.

On the one hand, he had worked hard for almost forty years to build his successful engineering career, and the idea of a flexible schedule and no stressful deadlines sounded refreshing. On the other, he realized that something about the idea of retiring scared him. His father had labored day after day until—with retirement just six months away—he'd suffered a stroke that had kept him in and out of hospitals until his death at age sixty-nine. Ever since, retirement had somehow been equated in George's mind with the end of usefulness, the end of productivity. The thought of his career being over astounded him. Really, it hit him hard.

But did he want to work himself straight into the grave? Was that his plan? Maybe the morning's curveball would allow him to pursue something different. Yet as he reread the highlighted words on the e-mail, he certainly had no idea what that "something different" might be. It seemed that all the breath had escaped from his lungs at once and didn't intend to come back anytime soon. What in the world was he going to tell Linda?

In need of another strong cup of coffee, George got up from his desk. As he entered the small cafeteria break room, he overheard two of his friends having a good-natured argument.

"Jim, I can't believe you are just going to sit on that cash and not get it invested," Fred was saying. "I've been trading oil stocks lately, and I'm making a killing."

Jim replied, "You're a much bigger gambler than I am. Who knows what's going to happen in the market? I read the other day that stocks are starting to look like they did just before the last crash. I don't want to get wiped out again."

"Listen," Fred said. "Some alarmist is always saying that. I'm taking advice from one of the greatest newsletters you've ever seen. You can't believe the track record this guy has for picking stocks. He can't seem to miss. If I keep this up, I'll be able to retire way before I had planned."

They both turned to George as he filled his cup.

"What do you think, George?" Fred continued. "Is the market going to keep going up, or is a crash just around the corner, like Jim thinks?"

George finished doctoring his coffee and stared blankly at his friends. "I don't know. How can anyone know for sure? It's way too complicated for me to figure out." He grimaced and put a hand on Jim's shoulder as he passed by. "I just know that I don't want to run out of money someday and have to live with either of you two."

They chuckled as he headed back out the door, but, as he turned the corner, he heard Jim say, "Wow, that was grim. Wonder what's gotten into George?"

When George returned to his office, he shut the door. Picking up his phone, he called his brother's number.

"Adam," he said when his brother answered, "I may have to retire early. I could use some investing advice."

"Are you sick? Is Linda OK?" Adam's normally gruff voice sounded pinched.

"No, no, nothing so bad as that. It's this darn merger. The lay-offs are right around the corner."

"You'll be OK, George. You've been there . . . what, twenty-five years? They're not going to just throw you out on your ear."

"Twenty-seven. I don't know, Adam. They're talking restructuring. Anything can happen. You know, it's multinational now—no personally knowing the guy you're going to can. Might be my whole department or just my projects . . ." He tapped his pen on the desk and cleared his throat. "So now they're talking about a forced early retirement."

"To you? You mean they already gave you the boot?"

"No, no, just an e-mail telling us to start considering the option."

"Well, take it from your older brother: the last option you want is early retirement." George heard a loud noise, as if Adam had slammed his hand on the desk. "Doggone it! Who do they think they are, pushing you off the retirement cliff? It's just like these young execs to think someone a little older has lost his usefulness. Like they have all the new knowledge and you're obsolete."

"Wow." George didn't quite know how to respond to Adam's unusual show of emotion. He rubbed his thumb across his chin as he considered his words. "I knew you had hit some bumps," he said, "but aren't you enjoying retirement? You had all those plans . . ."

The phone line hummed through Adam's silence as George gave his brother a minute to gather himself. "I messed it up, George," Adam finally said.

"What do you mean, you messed it up?" George asked. "Sure, you took a pretty big hit when the market crashed, but you've always been good at investing. I bet your holdings will be back where they were by the end of the year. Even if they aren't, you were set so well—I'm sure you can get by with a little less."

"No, George. I really messed it up." Adam's voice dropped so low that George had to increase the volume on his phone. "We have to find a buyer for that home we started building."

"What? What happened, Adam? You were so sure."

"I panicked when everything took a nosedive. I sold out at the bottom and was too afraid to buy back in as the market started picking up again. As a result, I lost a lot of money, and our income from investments has really taken a hit." He paused. "And I guess I should also confess that I haven't been stomping the pavement trying to find consulting jobs just because I've been bored. I've been doing it because we need the income. We're going to need it for a long time."

George was already exhausted—and it was only nine thirty in the morning. "Why didn't you tell us it was so bad? Linda and I would've paid for dinner last month."

Adam just sighed. "George, you tell them that you don't want their package. Who besides professional investors can figure out this fickle market? You're an engineer, not a broker. I say negotiate to keep your job no matter what. You don't want to end up like me."

After saying good-bye, George grabbed a pad of paper and divided the top sheet in half. Maybe it wouldn't be so bad. People retired all the time. Linda's retirement two years before from managing the office of a small medical practice had rejuvenated her. He tapped his pen on the pad and then wrote "golf," "traveling," and "freedom!" on the left side.

He tapped the pen once more. Then, on the right side, he wrote "Adam," followed by a dollar sign and an arrow pointing down. Then he crossed out "freedom!" He closed his eyes and rubbed his forehead. The market was so fickle. How could anyone figure out whether they had enough money to retire? And how would he manage all that money? Adam was right. He was an engineer, not a professional investor.

***

When he arrived home that night, George pulled his SUV into the garage and turned off the engine. He sat in the car, chewing on the inside of his cheek until the automatic garage light clicked off. As he removed the key from the ignition, his eyes were drawn to the back wall, still lit up by the headlights. Lining the rows of metal shelves were dusty tools, boxes of Christmas lights, and a trophy he had won years ago in a high-school art show. Memories clung to the old objects like ghosts. He remembered building his daughter's dollhouse and his son's backyard fort. He remembered the rosy cheeks and bright eyes of his now-grown children as he lit up the tree and house for the holidays each year. When had he grown old? Was he headed toward sitting as a dusty relic on a shelf of memories? When his father died, he hadn't been much older than George was now. Was this the beginning of the end?

The garage light clicked back on overhead as he opened the SUV door and climbed out. He hoped Linda had enjoyed her day more than he had. When he entered the house, the familiar aroma of onions and roast chicken warmed him. Linda sat with her back to him, writing out a check at the desk in their kitchen.

"For a moment there, I thought I was going to have to come out there and find you," she said.

George hung his coat on the hook by the door. "How was your mom today?"

His wife swiveled around in her chair, her brows knit together. "Mom woke up last night and got upset because it was dark and she couldn't remember where the bathroom was. The home health nurse said that either she forgot to leave the bathroom light on or Mom turned it off after one of her frequent trips. It took her a while to calm Mom down and bring her back to reality."

George nodded once and considered his words. "Do you think it's safe to keep letting her stay in her own home?" he asked.

"For now, while I can help, I still think it's fine." She smiled. The way her face could transform so quickly from concern to the well-earned laugh lines that framed her mouth and the corners of her eyes gave him comfort.

"Oh well," she said. "By the time I got there, she was ready to beat me at gin rummy. And look at this," she continued, reaching into a shopping bag and pulling out a plush dog with electronic buttons on its tummy. She stood and handed the animal to him. "I found the cutest little toy for Miranda. I thought I'd stock up on a few playthings so Susan doesn't have to cart the whole house over here every morning when I'm watching the baby."

George slid a chair out from the table and sank into it. He pushed a few of the buttons, and the dog started singing the alphabet and wiggling its ears. "Kinda fancy for a baby, isn't it?"

"Not for my grandbaby, it's not." Linda's hand found its way to her hip. "OK, out with it. What's wrong, George?"

He sighed. "I thought we had our future pretty well planned out."

"And . . . ?"

"The company is starting the restructure. I got an e-mail suggesting early retirement might be my only option."

Linda pursed her lips. "Well. That stinks. What does that mean?" She rescued George from the singing dog by taking it from him and sliding the off switch. "So they're not going to let you keep working until you're sixty-six?"

"I'm not sure yet. Maybe. Maybe not."

"OK," Linda said, sitting back down. "First of all, I'm really sorry, George. Second of all, what does that do to our plans? Without your full Social Security benefits and several more years' worth of savings, will we have the income we need?"

"I don't know, hon. There is so much to figure out." He took a deep breath and loosened his tie. "I thought we had a good plan. When you quit work a couple of years ago, it seemed like we would be OK if I could keep working until at least sixty-six."

Linda set the toy down. Her face softened. "It would be nice to have you around more."

"Not if you have to go back to work."

A flash of concern crossed her eyes. "Is that really a possibility?"

George ran his hand through his hair and sighed. Was it truly a possibility? How could he predict now what would happen in the future?

"I talked to Adam today," he answered. "He started consulting because they don't have enough income, not because he was bored."

"I wondered about that." Linda tore the check she had written out of the checkbook and slid it into a payment envelope. "This is next month's payment to the home health nurse for Mom," she said, and she licked the envelope. "You didn't answer my question, George. Do I need the agency to schedule more shifts for Mom next month? Do I need to tell Susan I can't watch the baby?"

He shook his head. "No, not next month. We have a little time."

"But you think I'm going to need to find a job?"

"All I know, Linda, is that my stomach is in knots over this. Adam thought he was set. How in the world can people know whether they will have enough put aside to live reasonably? How can we be sure we won't run out of money before we run out of health and time?"

The oven timer beeped.

"Well," Linda said, "there's no point worrying over something we can't fix right at this moment. Your stomach may be in knots, but mine is hungry, and I can't think when I'm hungry. Let's eat. You can tell me the details over dinner."

Later that night, by the time George finished reading over his asset spreadsheet for the twenty-second time and set the file on his nightstand, his wife was already settled into the pillows. She lay there, turned away from his reading light, and he watched her back rise and fall with her soft breathing. He envied her ability to fall asleep despite the uncertainty that kept his mind churning.

As he reached to turn off his light, she rolled sleepily to face him. "If you do decide to retire, and I don't have to go back to work, what are you going to do with your time?" she asked. "You can't just putter around the house."

"What else is there?"

Linda returned to her side, mumbling, "I'm not sure I could stand you underfoot *all* the time. You can play more golf, and we can take some of the trips we've been dreaming about, but what then? Eventually, you'll be bored."

George had to admit that he really didn't know what he would do. Already he could see boredom around the next corner. All he had ever done was work. He liked the challenge and the growth work offered. He didn't really have many hobbies or great passions to pursue. The thought of all that free time—coupled with all his money fears—really scared him. As he struggled to fall asleep, staring at the ceiling, thinking about how to make the money work and what he would do with the rest of his life, he realized that he was determined to keep working.

The next morning, as he looked through the newspaper, he told Linda his thoughts. "You know, at the heart of it, I'm a design engineer," he explained. "I've done a good job, and my work has made a difference for the company and for other people—at least, I think it has. I'm not sure how I'll define who I am if I no longer can call myself a design engineer."

Linda listened quietly as she broke eggs into a skillet. After a moment, she said, "It must be hard to feel forced out of your career. At least I got to choose my timing. I was ready to leave. Of course, now even that could be up in the air." The eggs sizzled and popped. "What about looking for a job with another company or doing something completely different?"

At the table, George folded down the corner of the paper and peered quizzically at his wife. "I'm sixty-three years old. What are you talking about?"

"Last night I had the feeling you would decide to keep working rather than retire now, but I've started wondering if this might be your chance."

George looked back at the paper. "My chance for what?"

"For branching out. For finding your calling."

"My calling? I've found it. I'm a design engineer. That's why I switched companies all those years ago. I like it. I'm really good at it." He turned to the business section, mumbling as he did so, "And who's going to hire a sixty-three-year-old design engineering has-been now?"

Linda shoved him gently with her hip as she set a plate of eggs and toast in front of him next to his coffee. "You're not a has-been." She paused on her way back to the stove. "Listen. I know you love the process of creating designs and solving difficult challenges. But be truthful. Does what you design for your firm make you want to get out of bed in the morning?"

George frowned. "I think I've been pretty successful. I've worked on some great projects, raised a terrific family, and all that."

"I'm not saying you haven't."

He sighed and put the paper down. "Then what are you saying? Now you want me to go galloping off after some fantasy? At my age? I thought you liked the status quo."

"I'll go over the budget this week. We have a lot in savings. There should still be a nice retirement package—"

"It's not enough," George snapped. "I've read everywhere that you need way over a million dollars to retire comfortably. I just don't think we're there."

"I really don't like the idea that the company can be so in charge of our lives," Linda replied, "either by making you retire just because they say it's time or by—what's the alternative? Making you move departments at their whim? Demoting you so you lose benefits you've already earned?"

"Some things just can't be helped, Linda. We're obviously not ready for me to retire, and I don't want to risk ending up short. And I certainly don't want you to have to go back to work just so I can take some retirement package."

Linda didn't respond. She filled her own plate, sat down, and silently buttered her toast. With her fork, she cut her eggs into bite-sized pieces. Then she began cutting those into even smaller bites.

George stopped eating and looked at his wife. "What do you want me to say, Linda? I get out of bed. I go to the office. I do my work. We can pay the bills. I'm satisfied. Who wants to spend their whole life at the office? Not anyone I know, but it's what you're supposed to do."

"But if you retired, maybe—"

"Lin, this whole retirement thing is great in theory . . . but I have no idea how we would make ends meet with no income. People are living longer, inflation just keeps increasing prices, and you never know when the market will nosedive again. It's too risky. I just need to stick it out, even if it means a demotion. We can save a lot with an extra few years of working."

Linda put her fork down. "My friend Martha, the one who volunteers with me at the clinic, was saying last week that her husband generally comes home from work in his best mood of the day."

"So now you're saying I'm grumpy?"

"No, I'm saying I think your job sometimes drains you more than it fills you up. When I've spent the day volunteering at the free clinic or with Mom, I come home tired but full. I'm satisfied.

I feel the joy of being well spent. I hardly ever felt that way when I was working, even though I loved my job. If you retired, maybe you could find that special something now instead of later." She dabbed at the corner of her mouth with her napkin.

George sighed.

"I just want you to enjoy life with me now," Linda added. "Who knows what will happen around the corner?"

The hallway clock chimed the hour. George stood up and carried his plate to the sink. "Well, I don't know how playing golf and fishing every day would help us keep afloat financially, but I guess our grocery bill could get cheaper."

Linda didn't respond. The smile he loved had gone into hiding.

Already, this problem was causing tension between the two of them. What would happen when money actually got tight?

"I'm meeting Dave for lunch to go over the plans for the new church building. Maybe I'll get his opinion," he grumbled.

The corner of her mouth lifted a bit. George tossed her the dishtowel, saying, "Here. I'm late." He gave her a kiss on the cheek and grabbed his coat from the hook. "Don't get too many ideas. I don't even know what kind of deal the company has in mind yet."

At work that morning, George struggled to stay focused on his design. While double-checking some project parameters on-line, he entered a search for "retirement strategies" and browsed several of the thousands of hits listed. When he refilled his coffee in the break room, he picked up a financial publication lying by the coffeepot and searched for the next quarter's stock forecast. As he checked his cell phone for e-mail, he noticed the Dow index had dropped. Would checking stocks become an obsession now, a daily pattern?

At noon, George left the office and met Dave for lunch. Dave was not only the senior pastor at George and Linda's church but also a good friend. As they ate, the two spread the church's blueprints out on the table and reviewed them.

"So you think that if we put the new connecting stairway in the adjoining alcove, rather than here in the center, we'll save money?" Dave asked.

George swallowed a bite of burger and pointed to the long, south-facing wall of the church. "We know we're going to have to modify this structural wall," he said. He slid his finger to another line, perpendicular to the first, that indicated an interior wall. "But this wall is structural too. If you put the stairs in the center, you'll go right through the header that runs across this opening. If you place the stairwell in the alcove instead, you'll avoid having to deal with the second structural wall."

Dave put more dressing on his salad and tossed it with his fork. "The architect won't like us messing with the symmetrical balance of his design."

George shrugged. "He has the luxury of working with business income rather than donor contributions."

"Oh, I know it makes fiscal sense," Dave said, smiling. "I just dread taking the plans back to him one more time."

The server laid the bill on the table as she walked by. George slid it toward his plate. "At least ask the contractor what the cost difference would be. If it's not enough to worry over, you won't have to incur the architect's wrath. If it is, you'll have solid numbers to prove your point."

"I knew there was a reason we needed to have lunch," Dave said. "You always help me bring the important details into focus."

"Apparently it's easier to see what someone else needs to do."

Dave looked at him thoughtfully. "Something eating at you?"

George picked up the bill and checked the amount. "Oh, you know. I'm having to relook at some of our retirement plans, and I'm not sure which way to go." He slipped his credit card in the check holder and gave it back to the server.

Dave leaned back in his chair. "Having trouble finding those solid numbers?" He crossed his arms in front of his chest. "I'm paying the tip, by the way."

George grinned. Punctuating his words in the air with his last french fry, he said, "Here's a tip: french fries taste better than salad." He ate the fry. "Is it even realistic to say 'solid numbers' and 'retirement' in the same sentence? I guess it really boils down to this: Can I take an early retirement package without having to find some part-time job or force Linda to go back to work? I don't want her to give up the great things she's doing. On top of that, can I figure out what I'm going to do with my time to make my retirement as fulfilling as Linda's has been? And we have to be able to do all this and move into the unknown future without going broke." He shook his head. "Time and money. It seems those questions are two sides of the same coin. How do you answer one without knowing the other?"

"Maybe you could use some life coaching," Dave said.

George stopped in the middle of signing the credit-card slip and looked over the rim of his glasses at Dave. "You too? I may have to rethink buying lunch."

"You have something against life coaching?"

"I'm sixty-three years old. Most of my career is behind me. Maybe if there had been life coaches when I'd just started working, I'd have bitten." He finished signing the slip. "I just need to figure out this money thing."

Dave set down his fork and wiped his mouth with his napkin. "A lot of people tell me that as they get nearer to retirement age, they feel a little lost with the sudden changes retirement can bring." He pulled a few bills from his wallet and laid them on the table for the server. "Let me give you an example from the Old Testament. At the beginning of the Book of Joshua, the Israelites are preparing to cross the Jordan River and seize control of the Promised Land. But after 430 years of slavery in Egypt and another 40 years spent wandering around in the desert, these people had no experience in war or in conquering other nations. They were entering an entirely new phase of life, and they felt completely unprepared—way out of their comfort zone. Sound familiar? God knew how they were feeling, so he promised to provide wisdom and direction. He told them that if they honored him and followed his lead, 'Then you will know which way to go, since you have never been this way before.'" Dave leaned his whole body forward on his elbows. "I'm just saying that, for you, maybe retirement will be like crossing that Jordan River. There's a whole passel of opportunities for you to conquer and tend to on the other side—if you find some wisdom to help you evaluate what your promised land should be."

George sat back and scrutinized his friend's face. The same passion that showed when Dave preached danced in his eyes now. For the first time since he read that e-mail the day before, George could feel a glimmer of hope rising up within himself. Could there be a promised land for him after retirement—a way to remain useful and active, pursuing new challenges? The challenges that appealed to him at the moment all seemed tied to his job or to a job just like it.

"OK," he said. "You and Linda win. I'll play this game. But how in the world do I find that wisdom? If I haven't figured it out by now, is it realistic to think I can make up my mind in the next few weeks?"

A familiar grin spread across the pastor's face. He nodded once. "You're looking at this like it's the end," Dave said. "Maybe this is just the beginning of something better and more exciting. I've found that one of the best ways to plot the path forward is to look back at where you've come from. Maybe start there, and I'll see if I can drum up some more resources for you."

George pushed his chair back from the table, reached across, and shook Dave's hand. "Thanks," he said. "I guess it can't hurt."

2

The Past Is Prologue

"These days people seek knowledge, not wisdom. Knowledge
is of the past. Wisdom is of the future."

—*Vernon Cooper, Native American elder*

George has found himself at an important crossroads, hasn't he? Like most of us, he has discovered that life is a series of midcourse corrections we make as we try to plan for the future. Is he on the right road? Should he have turned off several miles back? Where does he go from here?

George and his pastor, Dave, have hit on a critical issue that many people face in their fifties and sixties. Most people don't want to simply retire as their parents did. They want to stay engaged and perhaps be even more productive or have an even greater impact than they did while working full time. As Bob Buford writes in his book *Halftime*, today's retirees want to move from "success to significance."[2] The problem is that most of us don't know how to prepare for this second part of life.

To prepare adequately, we need to be able to answer two fundamental questions. One is about our time: "What can I do with my time to feel productive and make an impact?" The other is about our money: "How can I afford to stop working and not run out of money?" As George has discovered, these emotionally charged questions are two sides of the same coin. You can't really plan the one without knowing the answer to the other.

We will get back to George shortly. In the meantime, let's look at the framework he will use to tackle the question about significance. We will focus on the money side in the second half of the book, but George has some work to do on his future plans first.

The Encore Curve

Each person's life is lived in stages, and retirement can represent a whole new life stage if we plan it right. Consider the curve in the graph below.

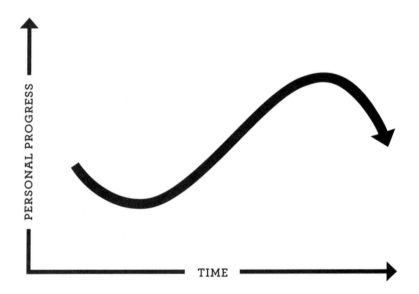

Think of this curve as depicting your life history—your Personal Progress Curve. In engineering, this curve is often called a "sigmoid curve" and is used to measure productivity over time. The first part of the curve shows your early adult years as you are getting your act together. The second part, which slowly rises over time, is the time in your life in which you are most productive and successful. Now notice the top of the big curve, where it turns downward and begins to decline. This is where many retirees find themselves. They have grown tired and lost some focus, and their life slowly goes into decline.

But what if there were a way to turn that declining curve back into upward progress? In this second graph, I've drawn in an upward curve at the point of decline.

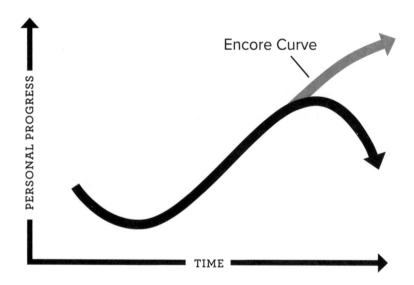

This is the curve I want to help you design for your retirement: a new curve that extends upward, not downward. I call this the Encore Curve because it represents our curtain call, when we close out our show with the very best we have to offer.

Imagine a great concert. When the band walks off the stage at the end, the audience rises to its feet and demands an encore. The band members then come back out and perform their greatest, most memorable hit—the song that made them famous. They save their best for last. This is what we want our retirement time to be: a time when we package up all the best that we have to offer and leave it on the stage as the audience roars for more. The Encore Curve represents how you want to live the rest of your life.

Through the next few chapters, with George's help, you will examine your life experience in the context of this model and discover specific personal factors that will help you design a new curve for your future. I hope you can discover how to replace the decline you may be feeling with a renewed excitement.

It has been my experience that a person's life curve begins to spiral downward when he or she is no longer able to visualize an exciting future. This is really the point at which a person's future tends to shrink and to become less inviting than his or her past. As we age, our futures obviously become shorter in terms of time. However, they need not become smaller in terms of significance. Our days ahead can still become even more significant than those that have passed. They can be packed with meaning, enjoyment, and impact. That's the point of the Encore Curve. Regardless of age, we all want to build meaningful futures in which we are doing what we are passionate about, using our greatest strengths and gifts, and making a difference for other people and for our world. The Encore Curve is the point at which we take the best of who we are and refocus on where we want to go.

Review, Repackage, and Repurpose

Returning to what Pastor Dave said earlier about the Israelites, we recognize that we all want the wisdom to know which way to go when we've never been that way before. When we start something new, such as retirement, it's always nice to have someone with experience to show us the way. We've all heard that experience is the best teacher and that practice makes perfect. You have probably also heard this Shakespearean line: "What's past is prologue."[3] For our purposes, that means our personal history sets the context for our future.

Therefore, we will take a three-step approach to creating our own Encore Curve: review, repackage, and repurpose. First, I'm going to show you how to review and reexamine your past experiences, as well as how to discover what has worked in your life and what hasn't. We will call this our "personal wisdom." Second, I want to help you organize what you've learned from this examination and repackage it into workable, life-focusing tools. In the third step, you will learn to repurpose what you have learned and to build a new game plan for life that will let you use your best lessons from the past and minimize your worst experiences. You will use this game plan to empower your retirement and build your own Encore Curve.

Surfing the Curve

To better understand what happens to a person's work life or career, let's draw our own curve and make some assumptions. Our Personal Progress Curve attempts to measure how a person's success pattern changes over time.

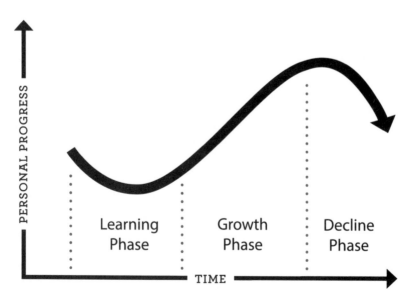

In the first stage—the Learning Stage—we are just starting out in a career. For most of us, this is a time of experimentation as we find which career niche we fit. Some people know immediately which career path they want to pursue, but many of us need time to figure it out. Think about when you were in this stage. At times, it seemed as though a fog had settled around you. Some people stayed in the fog and never found their way. Others eventually emerged from the fog with a clear direction, like George did when he changed companies. Then there were the fortunate few who were never in a fog and always saw a clear path unfolding before them.

As we find our niche and start to make progress, we enter the Growth Stage. This is where we begin to make our mark and where we spend most of life. For George, this stage has been in design engineering, the place where he felt he'd found his calling working on special design projects. The Growth Stage often seems to involve a compounding effect as we learn and improve new skills and then apply what we have learned to create more success. This is the stage in which we learn from experience, develop our personal wisdom, and see what works and what doesn't work in our lives.

There are some dangers in the Growth Stage. We often feel forced to follow someone else's agenda—whether that someone is a boss, a corporation, or an industry. Success does not always follow our hard work. We may fall into a rut and suddenly find ourselves unhappy and bored or overworked and underappreciated. As the saying goes, we run the danger of climbing a ladder of success only to find it leaning against the wrong wall. Many of us cycle through several Growth Stages as we change careers.

The third stage in the curve is the Decline Stage. We normally imagine this stage coinciding with retirement, but the Decline Stage can occur at any time. Maybe we just grow bored with what we are doing and start to lose energy. Perhaps we don't have the desire to work as hard as we once did or realize that we have not progressed as quickly or as far as we thought. Maybe our health has begun to decline; maybe chasing success has harmed our family relationships. Perhaps we have been extremely successful but now find we don't have the same drive. Whatever the reason, we feel ourselves slowing down in this third stage, and we want to make a change. This is where most retirees find themselves. As I said earlier, the Decline Stage can be dangerous because we can lose focus and motivation and fall into habitual patterns of regret, laziness, or just not knowing what to do next.

The exciting thing for you, however, is that you can then reach a new stage—an Encore Stage—in which you can assemble all the experience, passion, and skills of your previous stages and repackage them into a new plan for the next part of your life. Remember: if past is prologue, then discovering your personal wisdom is the first step in defining where you want to go with the rest of your life.

Older but Wiser

Before we begin designing your own Encore Curve, let's look at another concept: wisdom. Eighteenth-century philosopher Søren Kierkegaard helped define how life unfolds when he said, "Life can only be understood backward, but it must be lived forward." As we move forward to design the future, our greatest guide is our own past experience—our personal wisdom.

You may believe that much of your career path has just happened to you and that you haven't made conscious decisions about its direction. Life seems this way to many people, and at times we feel like spectators subject to the agendas of others. Now, as we face retirement, we are in danger of living in the past and not realizing that our life experiences have prepared us for an exciting future. Many of us have become victims of our past because we've either focused on our regrets and failures or tried to relive our victories and triumphs. We face the danger of letting our memories outweigh our vision.

I remember hearing a speech years ago at an industry meeting. The theme of the speech was that, as adults, we often feel as though we must either live up to or live down who we were in high school. This is a great example of living in the past, which is the danger of aging and retiring. Understanding your personal wisdom by examining your past experiences, however, can become your best guide for defining an exciting future. So let's look at this concept of wisdom a little closer.

> Now, as we face retirement, we are in danger of living in the past and not realizing that our life experiences have prepared us for an exciting future.

Your Wisdom Is Being Hijacked

One of the reasons we often feel as though we have lost control of our lives or fear moving forward with confidence is the fact that we now live in what I call a "sound-bite world." We are bombarded with noise and clutter that impact how we make decisions. All of our important input now comes in the form of sound bites that try to crowd each other out. Data is overwhelming the wisdom in our lives.

Facebook, Twitter, Instagram, television, the Internet—all the messages we receive wage a war to grab our attention. They compete to permanently imprint themselves on our minds to the exclusion of all other competing agendas. The advertising industry calls it "share of mind." You and I feel it as stress and confusion. In fact, more than one observer has said that we have become "grazers" of information. We graze on the junk food of data and never take the time to dig deeper for the healthy stuff of wisdom.

It is estimated that the *New York Times* contains more information on a daily basis than a person living two hundred years ago would encounter in his or her whole life. We humans are not prepared to live in this kind of world. We don't have the training to effectively cope with such an onslaught of data. We don't have the experience to sort through all the competing messages and make wise decisions. Data is robbing us of wisdom, making us feel stressed, and forcing us to feel as though we are falling further behind each day. This addiction to data is depriving many of us of a clear vision of our future.

We need a built-in filter that will allow us to either ignore all this input or process it and make it useful. We need a system to help us move from data to wisdom. We need a realistic foundation from which we can make intelligent, unemotional decisions. To help build this foundation, let's examine a model of the kind of input we use to make decisions.

Look at the following illustration. In information science, the DIKW Hierarchy tells us that we actually receive and process input from four different levels or sources: data, information, knowledge, and wisdom. Each one develops indirectly from the preceding level of input, and each is used in a different way. The further we travel down the DIKW line, the greater our understanding becomes.

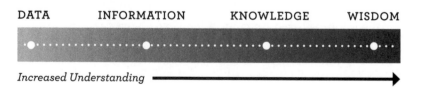

DATA   INFORMATION   KNOWLEDGE   WISDOM

Increased Understanding ⟶

First and most basic is *data*. Data is raw, uncorrelated pieces of information. Data is sound bites. Data is useful for only minutes because it changes constantly. It is just the facts—but without context, it is meaningless. Since we are talking retirement, let's use investing to illustrate what I mean. For example, you might read that the Dow Jones Industrial Average closed at 15,000. Without context or correlation to anything else, that data is basically meaningless. It is just a piece of communication that becomes obsolete almost instantly.

Second is *information*. This is data in context. It is data that has been analyzed and correlated, so it can remain useful for a longer period of time. For instance, if you know that the Dow is now 15,000 and that it was only around 1,000 back in 1982, or 7,000 only a few years ago, then you have a sense of comparison. Information becomes more meaningful than raw data.

The third level is *knowledge*. Knowledge is information that has been analyzed and proven by practical experience. For example, if you had invested in stocks in 1982 (when the Dow was around 1,000) and watched your investment grow, you would have a better understanding of how the market worked over that period of time. You might even be able to make some meaningful assumptions about what to expect from your investments in the future. Knowledge is slower to become obsolete and can therefore be used to make decisions and take action.

Finally, there is *wisdom*, which rarely becomes obsolete. In fact, wisdom becomes enhanced with the passage of time. It is the practical application of knowledge with predictable outcomes. It allows us to apply past lessons to the future. For our purposes, your personal wisdom is based on your unique experiences and the unique situations to which you apply your knowledge. As you begin to plan where you want to go in the future, it is imperative you discover the wisdom you have compiled so far.

	DATA	INFORMATION	KNOWLEDGE	WISDOM
CHANGE	Rapid, Constant · · · · · · · · · · · · · · · · Slow			
MENTAL STATE	Stress · Calm			
DECISIONS	Confused · · · · · · · · · · · · · · · · · Clarity			
EMOTIONS	Fear · · · · · · · · · · · · · · · · · Confidence			
VALUE	Low · High			
	NEGATIVE ⟵—————————⟶ POSITIVE			

Look at the DIKW model above and you will see the emotional dangers of constant dependence on data instead of wisdom. Data changes rapidly and constantly, creates stress, produces fear and confusion, and therefore has low value. Wisdom, on the other hand, is slow to change, has a calming effect, produces clarity and confidence, and thus has a very high value. Compare, for example, the psychology of the day trader trying to make minute-by-minute bets with that of the long-term investor who has a carefully thought-out game plan. The former is usually in emotional turmoil, while the latter is more calm and assured.

Wisdom and Time

Now look at the following illustration. Scientists tell us that there is a correlation between the DIKW spectrum and time. For our purposes, we can see that data, information, and knowledge all relate to the past. They are ways that we capture and analyze past events. Wisdom, on the other hand, relates to the future. As we plan our future, we want to capture the data, information, and knowledge specific to us. But staying focused on the Data–Information–Knowledge part of the spectrum is like living in the past. The Wisdom end of the spectrum is what allows us to translate the Data–Information–Knowledge from the past and make decisions for the future.

So how do we get there? When we integrate our DIKW understanding into our sigmoid curve, we discover a correlation. As you can see in the following illustration, the Data–Information–Knowledge component helps us plot the curve; it gives us points of reference to see the shape of our past personal progress. The wisdom component, on the other hand, interprets the unique experience and situation to which our knowledge is applied; it allows us to project into the future a richer, deeper, and more fulfilling curve—the Encore Curve—even when the future is smaller than the past in terms of time. Wisdom is knowing how to live so that life works the way we want it to. With proper planning, our Encore Curve future can even be more exciting, more productive, and more impactful than our past.

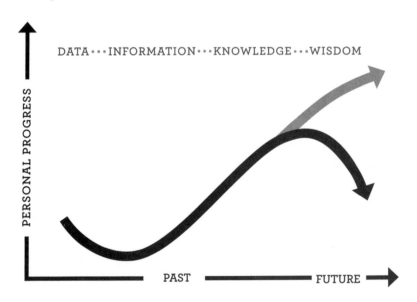

Finding the Wisdom in Our Backpacks

Most of us have spent life toting around an invisible backpack into which we place all of our experiences: our great triumphs as well as our crushing disappointments, regrets, and failures. We have thrown all of these experiences into our backpack, and it has grown heavy. Most of the stuff we keep lugging around in there, however, is just data, information, and knowledge. It is the combined experience of our past, but it is often not the kind of wisdom that we can use for the future.

Who says we have to drag the entirety of our backpack into the future? All this past data weighs us down. One of the keys to creating an exciting Encore Curve future—a future that has even more meaning and impact than your past—is to learn how to mine those past-based Data–Information–Knowledge rocks in your backpack and extract the gems of Wisdom. Once you do this, you can then give yourself permission to take only the Wisdom into your future and leave the backpack in the corner, where it can no longer hold you back.

Throughout the rest of this book, you will encounter exercises and worksheets that will coach you through the process of planning your future. You will receive the most benefit from this book by completing these exercises as you go—or by at least coming back to them as you can and working through them sequentially. To start, I want you to imagine your own Personal Progress Curve and then answer the questions below. For now, you are looking for an overview of your past. (You will examine the contents of your backpack more closely in chapter 4.)

At the end of this chapter and every chapter that has an exercise, you will find a worksheet that gives you a place to write down some of your answers right here in this book. Please also visit EncoreCurve.com/worksheets for full-size worksheets and additional help.

Personal Progress Curve Exercise

Think back over your life, and divide it into the three phases of the Personal Progress Curve: the Learning Stage, the Growth Stage, and the Decline Stage. (You may find that you went through several of these curves as you changed jobs or switched careers. It's OK to create more than one curve, and it's a good detail to notice about your past.) Then answer these questions:

- When did each stage of your curve start and end?
- What were the driving forces that caused each stage to transition to the next?
- Have you experienced more than one curve during your life? If so, how many? What driving forces made you jump to the next new curve?
- If you could travel back in time to one or two of those change points, what would you like your "present-day self" to say to your "yesterday self"?

Now let's rejoin George as he begins to discover his own successes and frustrations and how they impact his plans going forward.

PERSONAL PROGRESS WORKSHEET
ANALYZING THE CURVE

Look back at your life in terms of the Personal
Progress Curve. Try to divide them into phases of the curve.

When did each section of your curve begin and end?

LEARNING

GROWTH

DECLINE

What were the driving forces that caused each section to transition to the next?

1. _____

2. _____

3. _____

4. _____

5. _____

Full-size worksheets are available at EncoreCurve.com/worksheets

PERSONAL PROGRESS WORKSHEET
ANALYZING THE CURVE

These questions are a continuation of the Personal Progress Worksheet.

Have you experienced more than one curve during your life? If so, how many and what driving forces made you jump to the next new curve?

If you could travel back in time to one or two of those change points, what would you like your "present-day self" to say to your "yesterday self"?

Full-size worksheets are available at EncoreCurve.com/worksheets

3

What Lies Ahead

"The future ain't what it used to be."

—*Yogi Berra, baseball manager*

Saturday after lunch, George was sitting at a small table in the glassed-in porch, enjoying the sunshine that hinted at spring. Lost in thought, he didn't hear the sliding door or Linda's footsteps, so he jumped when she tossed a stack of advertisements on the table and sat down.

She chuckled. "Penny for your thoughts."

He cleared his throat. "Oh, I discovered some old feelings I had forgotten."

She rested a hand on his knee. "Care to share?"

Beyond the large windows, two squirrels chased each other across the yard. George rubbed his brow. "One day, during my senior year in high school, my father sat me down for a talk. I had filled out an application for an art school as well as for college, and he wanted to straighten me out about that."

She nodded. "He could be a bit hard-nosed."

He grimaced. "You think? Well, he said that I was eighteen now and needed to step into my future like a man. He said art school was a selfish, childish dream. I should be proud to go into engineering, as he had done, and make a good living."

"Ah," Linda said. She flipped through the ads, scissors in hand, to find what she was looking for. "So engineering was . . . ?"

"Something I was good at but not passionate about at the time."

"Huh. I thought you loved engineering. You mean you felt pushed into it?"

George considered this. "More like cut off from what I enjoyed most. I didn't hate engineering. But when I graduated . . . I don't think I ever told you that Dad set up that interview for me with Mammoth—his company. From the beginning, I wasn't sure it was the right choice for me, but we were getting married, and Dad pushed hard in favor of the stability and opportunity of going with a large, national firm."

He could see Linda processing this information as she began clipping coupons from the paper. "Your father could be overbearing at times, but all in all, it wasn't bad advice," she said.

He shrugged. "No, of course not. Especially not at first. It was a solid job offer, and they invested years in training me. That's really where I learned to love design, combining my engineering skills with creativity." As he began straightening the little piles of glossy print rectangles she was creating, he noticed a coupon for Hamburger Helper in the stack. Maybe George didn't know if he liked the direction his career was headed, but he was *sure* he disliked the direction of dinner.

"The thing is," he continued, "you couldn't specialize and stay in one place with them. You had to keep moving up the ladder. Dad thought that was great, but that's when I felt like I had reached a dead end there. I was bored, I was overloaded with administrative tasks and meetings, and the travel cut deep into our family time." When Linda wasn't looking, he slid that Hamburger Helper rectangle out of the pile and off the table with the practiced sleight of hand he used to entertain his eldest granddaughter. "There've been times in my current job that I've enjoyed one project less than another, but I've never felt so far out of my niche and away from my calling as I did at Dad's firm. And yet what did Dad say when I quit? He said I'd be a fool to give up a solid pension with a big company to work for a smaller firm. And here I am, a fool." He picked up a page that Linda had left uncut. "You didn't cut out the ice cream coupon," he said.

She patted his rounded middle. "You don't need ice cream. Plus, that brand is overpriced." She scanned through the next several pages, tipping her head the way she tended to do when she was thinking. "It's good that you're thinking about your past. It seems to me that understanding the past can give us some insight into our next steps. But I think it would be best to figure out what we can learn from those experiences rather than spend a lot of time dwelling on the things that we can't change."

"You're probably right. I guess this . . . this early retirement push just makes me feel like it's Dad all over again, taking away something I love to do and being proven right in the end."

Linda turned a couple of pages, then abruptly put the scissors down. "What did you want to do at art school?"

"Oh, that's ancient history."

"Humor me."

"I don't know, Lin. I think I fancied myself as someone who could draw well—"

"You can."

"Having some skill and having artistic talent are two different things."

"And you don't think you have talent?"

"I think Dad was right in that it wouldn't have paid the bills."

"Maybe, but I was asking about talent." Linda crossed her arms and studied him shrewdly. "If I know you at all, I'd bet you sent in the application anyway. Did you?"

"Maybe."

"And . . . ?"

He flushed slightly. "They accepted me, but what does that prove? It's been some forty years since then."

"It proves that some experts thought you had talent." The light had shifted, throwing traveling shadows across the table. "Do you still like to draw?"

George thumbed the edge of the stack of circulars, riffling through each page like a flipbook. "Some, but it doesn't catch my attention like it used to. It's more of a means to an end now—a launching pad for engineering ideas."

"Maybe that part of you is just a bit rusty from disuse."

"I'd need more WD-40 than you can buy, I think," he said. But despite himself, for the first time since he'd spoken with Pastor Dave, George felt that hope again, rising in his chest like a small gust of helium lifting his spirits. Was that passion for drawing still there, just stuffed away alongside the other dusty tools in his emotional garage? "And when did you start clipping coupons again?" he said. "You hated clipping coupons when the kids were little."

"Today," she said. "And I still hate it."

Outside, the frolicking squirrels tangled up around some stacked flowerpots, scattering the containers across the deck. Linda looked up at the noise and sighed. "Did I tell you the home health nurse called this morning? Mom couldn't remember how to use a fork at breakfast."

"I'm sorry, Lin. I know it's hard to watch her health and mind deteriorate right in front of you," George said.

Her frown seemed to flirt with hanging around, but it softened as she looked at him. "I know all this introspection lately probably appeals more to me than to you. But while I might approach it from more of a feeling perspective, with your analytical mind, I think you could look at it as an engineering problem that needs to be solved." She held her hand out, palm up, as if he were a naughty grandchild. "And I did see you take that coupon."

He placed the crumpled paper in her outstretched palm. "I guess I should avoid going into professional magic, then."

At that, her frown lost its battle. She smoothed out the rectangle and again placed it on her pile. Propping her elbows on the table, she rested her chin on her hands so that her face came closer to George's. Her brow furrowed above eyes that sought his.

"Do you know what I like most about volunteering at the free health clinic?" Linda asked. "I like helping people in need. And I can do that there without worrying about patient insurance or productivity or instituting all the new policies the government requires. Since I never got my nursing degree, I had to help people vicariously through paperwork and good management for all those years. Now I feel like I spend my day connecting with the actual people, holding their hands and giving them hope, showing them that someone cares."

Worry creased the space between her eyebrows. She exhaled a small puff of frustration as she blinked.

George glanced out the window, wondering if the sun was in her eyes.

"Honestly," she said, "I can't imagine having to give that up."

In spite of the solemn tone the conversation had suddenly taken, George felt Linda's passion ignite his little spark of hope. Whatever he decided about retirement, he would make sure she could keep her options open. He took her hand, which was resting under her chin, and stroked the back of it with his thumb. "We'll figure it out," he said. "I have an appointment with the head of Human Resources in a couple of days to see what financial choices we might have."

"Good," Linda said, picking up the scissors once again and resuming her task. "Because this money question and this time question seem as tangled up as those two stupid squirrels that just knocked over my pots."

"I guess the more information we can gather, the closer we will get to the answer," he said.

She nodded absently.

"Something else nagging at you, Lin?" George asked.

"Mom's going to need an extra shift added to her care, and I'm not quite sure her budget can handle it. We're going to need to fill in that gap for a while."

George thought about that for a second, then remarked, "I think we need to toss in a measure of faith that there really are some answers. I remember that passage that Dave quoted: 'Then you will know which way to go, since you have never been this way before.' That sure seems to fit where we are."

"George Wilson Morris," Linda chided. "Don't tell me you are beginning to see some hope and promise in the middle of all this. I thought you were the worrywart in the crowd."

"Well," George said, grinning, "between you and Dave, I don't stand much of a chance, do I?"

***

Sitting in the pew beside Linda the next morning, George was struck by the Scripture that Pastor Dave had chosen for the morning's sermon: "Forgetting what lies behind and straining forward to what lies ahead, I press on."[4] It was easy for George to see how this could apply to his own situation. He knew he was clinging to his current job and routine—and he knew that routine couldn't last forever. What would it take for him to strain forward and press on?

"The apostle Paul," Dave reminded them, "who wrote this text in the book of Philippians, had enjoyed superb credentials and standing in his community. If anyone had reason to brag for all he had accomplished, it was Paul. So why," he asked, "did Paul say to forget all that and look forward? There can be only one reason." Dave paused and let the rustling settle. "He considered his vision of his future to be more compelling than his past. Do you?"

George considered that question for all of half a second. He knew the answer was still no. He felt comfortable in his current job, but when his job ended—either now or in a few years—his future would hold nothing to excite him.

"Paul is speaking in the context of spiritual matters," Dave continued, "but the principle rings true in all facets of our experience. In the book *Good to Great in God's Eyes*, Chip Ingram writes about the importance of having big dreams that empower your future. Do you regularly entertain some big dreams? Or are you on autopilot, living a stagnant status quo?"

George shifted uncomfortably in the pew. When had he stopped dreaming? Linda was right. He enjoyed his work, but he had long ago stopped thinking about what more he wanted for himself, what meaningful goals he wanted to accomplish. What was he moving toward?

After his first thought—*finishing the Murphy project*—George drew a blank. He found himself unsettled. The Murphy project, an experimental water desalination process, intrigued him with its potential, but it was entirely defined by his company. George had little or no say in the future of that project—or any other projects, for that matter. To his surprise, he began to realize he would like to have more control over what he did. What would that look like?

George thought back to his conversation with Linda the day before. Over time, he had adopted his father's attitudes toward the value of art and responsibility. He realized now that he had never stopped to reevaluate that position. What if he pursued art again? Would that feel frivolous? He had already supported his family very responsibly, if not exactly as his father had wanted. Suddenly, he was realizing that, while his current job was enjoyable and good, it was not, as Linda had said, pull-you-out-of-bed good, not *I-must-do-this-one-important-thing* good.

He wondered again what pursuing art would look like for him. Did he really have passions that went beyond design engineering? Was there any room in engineering for that kind of passion? He hoped Dave wouldn't ask him about the rest of the sermon later, because his own thoughts were drowning it out. But little by little, he felt the boundaries of his future widening.

At the conclusion of the service, Linda leaned toward George as she gathered her purse and jacket. Loud enough to overcome the chattery din of people breaking out in conversation, she whispered in his ear, "Do you sometimes feel Dave writes his sermons just for us? He must keep a picture of us on his desk for inspiration."

George laughed. He was glad he wasn't the only one with that thought. They filed out through the center aisle toward the back, where Dave was greeting the departing congregants.

"How's your mother this week, Linda?" Dave asked as he reached to shake her hand.

"Still deteriorating, but feisty," she said, "and looking forward to our card game this afternoon, I think. So far, her memory loss has yet to affect her ability to lay down gin twice as often as me."

Dave chuckled. "I think I'd better tread carefully on my prayers for that one."

"Pray I keep losing for at least another year," she said, moving off to get a peek at a friend's newborn grandchild.

Dave then grasped George's hand firmly with both of his. "George, I want to thank you for your advice on the stairwell construction. The architect acknowledged that his design lacked sense fiscally, and he's made the changes."

"Glad to help," George said. "You've made more progress than I have, then."

"Oh, about that, George—your introspection the other day got me thinking about a coaching program I went through a couple years ago that really helped me get a handle on where I saw myself headed in the ministry and beyond. I dug up the worksheets we used. If you can wait until I'm through here, I can give them to you. I thought they might help you and Linda assess your strengths and passions and focus your thinking for your future."

"Absolutely," George said, moving forward and to the side so that he was out of the line. "Straining for what lies ahead, huh?"

The smile spread across Dave's face. "That's right, George," he said as he reached to shake the hand of the next person. "So you will know which way to go."

4

Two Kinds of Wisdom

"Advice is what we ask for when we already know the answer but wish we didn't."

—Erica Jong, American author

George and Linda are looking in the right places to discover their Encore Curve. As you can see, Linda has navigated much further into understanding her strengths, her motivations, and what gives her joy. George, on the other hand, has felt more often that circumstances and those close to him have pushed him to follow a certain path—a path he might not have chosen on his own. He's still unsure of what he wanted then and what he wants now.

To find your Encore Curve, you need to understand your own personal wisdom, a wisdom that says, "If my life is going to change, I want to change it on my own terms." You've spent much of your life moving with the flow of everything and everybody else, being pulled this way and that by your parents, school, job, career, and family. Now that you have a chance to restart, why not do so based on who you are rather than who everyone says you should be? When we talk about personal wisdom in this chapter and in this book, remember that personal wisdom is not "your wisdom for me"; it's "my wisdom for myself."

The Personal Progress Curve Exercise in chapter 2 was intended to help you begin thinking about where the seasons of your life landed on the curve. This overview may have begun to give you a sense of your personal wisdom. But to get a clearer understanding of how the data, information, and knowledge of your past can turn into a foundation of wisdom for your future, you must review the rocks in your backpack in greater detail. You must look at the granular level to determine which rocks are actually valuable gems.

> Now that you have a chance to restart, why not do so based on who you are rather than on who everyone says you should be?

As you dig deeper, you will discover that you have developed two kinds of personal wisdom over the years: Earned Wisdom and Learned Wisdom. Earned Wisdom goes beyond job and career issues. It is the life wisdom you have acquired by experiencing successes and failures. Learned Wisdom, on the other hand, is the wisdom you have been able to borrow from others in order to leverage it and use it as your own. Let's explore both sources of wisdom in greater depth.

Earned Wisdom Gives You Direction

Because each person has a unique experience of life, nobody has a better understanding of yourself than you do. We each have a unique combination of beliefs and values about our past experiences, our present situations, and our future goals, and this combination drives our behavior in a subconscious way. As we live, we learn more about our strengths and our passions.

The first kind of wisdom—Earned Wisdom—begins as we realize our own knowledge and insight and understand who we are and who we want to be. We call this Earned Wisdom because we earn it by enrolling in the School of Hard Knocks. Once we understand our Earned Wisdom, we begin to understand why we are who we are—and if we don't like what we see, we can begin to grow and change. We can also begin to make better conscious choices that line up with our strengths and our dreams.

Since your Earned Wisdom consists of those things that are unique about you as a human being at this point in time, it can act as a compass that will keep you pointed in your own direction. George once knew that artistic endeavors gave him a sense of accomplishment, but he let his father's bias turn him away from this knowledge. Eventually, though, his own personal wisdom compass steered him back in that direction through design engineering.

Successful living is very subjective. No one is better equipped to tell you how to make yourself happy than you are. For most of us, our past experiences help define who we are and what this subjective happiness looks like. Therefore, the images and interpretations of your past history that you carry can become either a launching pad for your future happiness or a millstone around your neck. So to obtain the most benefit from your past, you must look carefully at not only what you have experienced but also what you have learned as a result.

We are going to start rummaging around in your backpack and taking out rocks to examine. For some of us, this will be exciting and eye opening; for others, it may be difficult and painful. Regardless, do your best to explore your whole backpack, even the dark corners way down in the bottom. The only way to stop carrying some of those heavy rocks into your future is by pulling them out and giving them a good, hard look to discover their real value.

To clarify your Earned Wisdom, you need to ask two questions: "What happened to me?" and "What did I learn?"

Past Events: "What Happened to Me?"

As you read through this section, grab a pen and paper to record any ideas that come to you. These ideas will form the basic material for your next exercise.

Beginning from your earliest memory, think about the major events in your life in terms of the following three categories. Try to list at least two or three events in each category.

Family Relationships

My mother died when I was sixteen, and my father's new business venture collapsed at the same time. Three years later Dad remarried, but his new wife jealously wanted nothing to do with me, a somewhat rebellious teenager. So at nineteen, I found myself on my own, estranged from my family. Twenty-five years later, when his second wife died, my father and I reconnected. During the final few years of his life, we grew to become good friends. It took me years to understand that I hadn't been the problem. He never explained, but ultimately, he didn't have to. Looking back, I see that the estrangement forced me to grow up and actually protected me from my family's "craziness" in many ways. What was at the time a terrible and stressful situation really turned out to be one of the best things that could have happened to me.

Ongoing Situations

What type of family atmosphere were you raised in? Was it nurturing or negative? Violent or peaceful? Were strong patterns or values established that have stayed with you? What kind of attitudes were you taught about money? What were you taught about work and job-related circumstances? Were you, like George, taught that there was only one mature way to look at a potential career? Were you allowed to grow and expand, or were you held back and manipulated? What about your current family circumstances? Has a broken relationship left you crippled, or have you been fortunate enough to have a full and loving relationship with your family?

Try not to wallow in pity if your past has been less than perfect. Instead, consider what skills and strengths you might have gained as a result of your trials. If you feel that you have never been allowed to express yourself honestly, write down the thoughts or likes and dislikes about yourself that you've never spoken aloud.

List some of the ongoing situations in which you have found yourself. What good came out of them? What bad things did you experience? Have you tried to repeat these situations, or have you tried to avoid them?

Marking Events

Many of us can point back to specific events in our lives that have marked us since that time. Perhaps one was a devastating loss, such as the tragic death of a loved one or the destruction of belongings in a fire. For some, it was a spiritual awakening. For others, it was a watershed decision that has had long-lasting implications personally or financially—or, more often, both. George's decision to pursue engineering rather than art falls into this category. That decision led to both negative and positive consequences.

Events like these often help define who we are. Whether they appear to be positive or negative, we have to embrace them as part of our life story. Once you can accept these events as part of who you are, you can consider whether they might motivate you to move in a particular direction. Sometimes we find our passions by turning the negative into the positive and by using our own pain and knowledge to help others. Sometimes—like Sam in the example—we cannot overcome these events.

Think about the marking events in your life. Did they become permanent roadblocks, or did they motivate you to discover better things?

Sam and Vietnam's Mark

For my brother-in-law, the marking event was Vietnam. After trying college, he enlisted in the Marines and found himself in a firebase north of Da Nang. He reenlisted twice and stayed in the middle of battle for nearly three years, winning a field promotion and several high commendations. When he returned, he began to experience psychological and physical problems that shaped the rest of his life. He had severe environmental allergies from chemical exposure and was not able to retain long-term employment. He developed an antagonistic attitude toward the world as he searched for relief from his physical problems and his recurring nightmares and headaches. Sam's health and mental issues were certainly part of the reason that he passed away at the age of fifty-seven without really fulfilling any of his potential.

Influential People

Who has influenced your life? How have these people changed it? Are there people in your life who have been heroes? Are there others who have been villains—perhaps a tyrannical boss, a dishonest partner, or an abusive parent or spouse? Have these people become symbols for you to emulate or to avoid emulating at all costs? Perhaps the way others have handled their money has impacted you. Was it because they were wise, generous, or stingy? Spend a few minutes listing those heroes and villains in your life and describing their influence on you.

Past Experiences: "What Did I Learn?"

Revisiting past experiences and milestones can be either an exciting exercise or a debilitating one. In either case, if it is simply a trip down memory lane, then it is a futile effort. As Linda hinted to George, the important thing is to learn lessons from our experiences that we can carry with us into our real-world activities.

The interesting thing about the past is that we can constantly redefine it based on new insights. The lessons we learn today can help us look at our past with fresh eyes and derive new and different conclusions from it. If you are serious about defining your own agenda for the future, then understanding your past experiences is vital. Being a victim of your past robs you of full ownership of your future and makes you subject to whatever outside influences and forces are stronger than you at any given time.

If you made a list of some of the influential things from your past, begin to evaluate them. For instance, did you merely survive, or did you thrive? Examine each item on your list, and rank it on a scale ranging from "barely survived" at one end to "truly thrived" at the other end. Then ask yourself, "Why?" In other words, what factors in each influence caused your ranking?

> The interesting thing about the past is that we can constantly redefine it based on new insights.

These questions are based on the assumption that all of our lifetime experiences generally fall into two categories based on subconscious expectations. First, there are "things that worked"—situations that unfolded the way we expected or better. Second, there are times when "things did not work"—situations that failed to meet our expectations. Either way, we can find wisdom in examining them.

There is a scene in the movie *City Slickers* in which Billy Crystal's character is riding along, talking about life with his friends as they herd cattle. Crystal asks his companions about the best and worst days of their lives. One friend starts by describing his worst day, the day when he was a teenager and had to stand up to his abusive father to protect his family. Crystal listens to the heart-wrenching tale and then asks, "What was the best day?"

After some thought, his friend answers, "Same day."

Isn't that the way it is with life sometimes? Our worst experiences, when examined in the light of retrospective wisdom, may suddenly become the basis for some of the best things in life.

Backpack Exercise

Please find the condensed worksheet at the end of the chapter. You can also go to EncoreCurve.com/worksheets for a full-size worksheet and additional help.

We can learn as much from our failures as from our successes. In fact, sometimes our greatest failures will teach us more than our biggest successes. So as you do this exercise, I urge you not to think of your failures and disappointments as final. One of the things I have learned through years of counseling people is that we always have the ability to redefine our past and use it to power our future. Therefore, think of your past failures as fodder for future success. That's why the last question in this exercise mentions the opportunity to "do over." It gives you a chance to learn from each experience.

Revisit what you wrote down in the Personal Progress Curve Exercise (chapter 2) as the driving forces that pushed you from one stage or one curve to another. Then consider the influences and experiences of your past that you have just reviewed and ranked according to the "survived or thrived" scale in this chapter. With all these things in mind, answer the following questions on the work-sheet at the end of this chapter.

1. **What worked?** What were your biggest successes or the best periods of time in your life? Why do you consider each of these a success?
2. **What did not work?** What were your biggest failures or times of frustration or regret? Why do you consider each of these a failure?
3. **What would you do over?** If you could do anything differently, what would that be? Why would you want to redo each of these experiences?

Did you discover any new gems of personal wisdom? Are there any old rocks you can now put in the corner of the room and leave behind? Sometimes rough diamonds need a little polishing before we can recognize them as gems. Sometimes we can't let go of rocks that are dead weight. That's when we need a little Learned Wisdom to help us bring our Earned Wisdom into focus.

Learned Wisdom Leverages Others' Wisdom

When things don't work—as they often don't—we feel deflated, lose confidence, get angry, and have all sorts of other negative reactions. The problem comes when the "Things That Did Not Work" column continues to grow. We begin to adjust our standard of measurement, our ideal, to accommodate the continued disappointment. In times like these, we often need the intervention and objective viewpoint of Learned Wisdom. When our experiences are negative and we have reached the end of our Earned Wisdom, we need to seek out a good dose of wisdom from others whom we trust.

If Earned Wisdom is what we earn on our own from the experience of living, then Learned Wisdom might be defined as wisdom other people have earned that we then borrow for ourselves without actually earning it. Learned Wisdom is the expertise, experience, and wisdom of other people that is available for you to integrate into your own wisdom in order to increase your ability to make wise decisions.

Learned Wisdom Can Lead You from the Unknown to the Known

When you were a child, where were your monsters? My monsters were always in the attic or the closet. When I visited my Aunt Ruth, I had to sleep in an attic that had been converted into a spare bedroom. Right behind the bed was a door that opened into the remaining attic. I just knew there were monsters lurking in the darkness behind that door, waiting to get me as soon as I fell asleep. So, of course, I didn't sleep. I cried and pleaded until Aunt Ruth came up the stairs, turned on the light, and took me into the attic to examine it thoroughly. Only when I was convinced I was in a monster-free environment did I finally fall asleep.

Isn't it funny how some of our greatest fears are of the unknown? We dread certain things in life—failure, death, bad health, outliving our income, the loss of a loved one. But often, as soon as our fears are dragged into the light, they seem to evaporate or at least change into something we can handle. That is why it's important to tap into the experience of others, especially if those others have been through the exact thing we fear. They have the ability to open the attic door and help us explore the dark unknown. Their experience helps us move from the unknown to the known and from fear to confidence.

Sometimes it's as simple as George gaining hope from his wife's passion for her postretirement activities. She has seen the good side—the useful side—of retirement, and he can learn from her how to change his thinking. Learned Wisdom adds to, improves, and helps clarify your Earned Wisdom. It can lead you from the unknown to the known, alleviating fear, especially during stressful times. The Learned Wisdom of others is often the catalyst that moves us from disappointment to a new perspective.

Sources of Learned Wisdom

Numerous potential sources of Learned Wisdom are available to each of us. Some can be more beneficial than others, but, at different times, we might need all of them. Some are more personal; others are more objective. We need both of those aspects. The soundness of your source of wisdom is dependent not necessarily upon how objective it is but on how it lines up with the Earned Wisdom you have discovered so far. The less other people's agendas play into their advice to you, however, the greater the likelihood that you are gaining wisdom rather than simply more data.

Below is a list of potential sources of Learned Wisdom. These categories are not exhaustive, and a single person or resource could fill several of these roles. These may be people who have already influenced you, or they could represent people you need to include in your life right now to add wisdom to your current journey.

Stakeholders. These people have a personal interest in our decisions.

Trench Buddies. These people are going through similar experiences at the same time.

Survivors and Thrivers. These people have already been where we are going and lived to tell about it.

Experts. These people are third-party specialists in specific areas.

Coaches. These people are wise counselors or experts whom we seek out for ongoing consultation.

Stakeholders

Our most personal source of outside wisdom will invariably be those people who are the most interested in our journey. For you, perhaps that includes family members, close friends, business partners, and so on. For many of us, like George, our biggest stakeholder is our spouse. Your spouse has more to gain or lose from your journey than any other person in your life. Therefore, while this input may be the least objective, it probably carries the most weight.

Trench Buddies

We all need support systems around us, especially in times of stress and turmoil. Trench Buddies can range from formal support groups to friends who are in similar situations. They can be of enormous help as sounding boards and objective listeners, and they can help us gain perspective on our situation. But beware of advice from Trench Buddies. As a rule, they are in the same place as you. They may be leaning on you for wisdom even as you think you are leaning on them. Don't put yourself in a blind-leading-the-blind situation when you are seeking clear vision.

Survivors and Thrivers

Earlier, I suggested that you reflect on your past experiences in terms of "barely surviving" or "truly thriving." As you did so, I hope you gained some powerful insights about how handling past experiences has prepared you to handle future experiences. We often lament, "If I only had known then what I know now . . ." That's the power of tapping into the wisdom of someone who has been where you are going. You get to take lessons from that person's experience and borrow them to apply to your own. So far, George's brother Adam has merely added to the fear and data inundating George. But we will see in the next chapter how Adam's experience can add to George's wisdom. Whether in person, through biographies, or through other nonpersonal sources, seek out the wisdom of others who have been there, and use that wisdom as your own.

Experts

You've probably heard it said that an expert is just someone from out of town with a briefcase. But building a network of accessible people and resources with specific wisdom in specialized areas can boost your Learned Wisdom substantially. Dr. Gary Holmgren, in his book *Responsibility Factor*, advocates the idea that we need to surround ourselves with prequalified experts. He suggests that we each have areas of our lives in which we are not qualified to be the expert and that, in each of these areas, we need to identify wise specialists to whom we can go for help. He further suggests that when we are experiencing tension, stress, or anxiety, we should follow the wisdom of these specialists regardless of how we feel, because our chance of making judgment errors is magnified when we make critical decisions under stress.

Coaches

A coach is someone who can lead you from confusion to clarity, help train you in new skills, or help you improve strengths that you already have. In sports, a coach's job is to teach new techniques to his or her players and to help them improve on the skills they already possess. Personal and business coaching has become a growth industry. In your quest for Learned Wisdom, you may want to retain a coach whom you pay to help teach you, lead you, or advise you in your areas of need. A professional financial planner or investment advisor is the perfect example of this type of coach. These people have specialized expertise and can help you tailor a wise solution in an area where you may need help.

Learned Wisdom Enhances Your Strengths

Years ago, in a vain effort to ward off aging, I joined a health club and began working out. I thought I was making real progress—until I hired a personal trainer. Suddenly, with his help, I began getting better results in less time than I had by working out on my own. He taught me how to use the weight machines properly: how much weight to use, the proper settings, and the correct posture. He encouraged me to do more than I had been doing on my own. Leveraging Learned Wisdom is like hiring a personal trainer in any area you need. You may already be an expert in that area, but gaining the added insight and encouragement of others will propel your progress forward.

The categories of coach and expert do overlap, but the main differences between the two are time and distance. A coach is an expert who spends time developing you, training you, and teaching you in that discipline. A coach develops a closer relationship with you, taking personal responsibility to transfer wisdom; you and your coach are jointly committed to achieving and improving. In contrast, an expert comes and goes, dropping pieces of wisdom along the way without making sure the wisdom is transferred to the learner. The expert may not even ever meet the learner. In this sense, coaches can and should be experts, but experts are not necessarily coaches.

A coach is uniquely qualified to take your knowledge and help you translate it into *your* wisdom. Remember our premise that information and knowledge are about the past, and only wisdom is about the future? A coach helps us apply knowledge to our particular situation and create wisdom we can use for our future.

What Happens When We Ignore Learned Wisdom?

Because his father's opinion overshadowed the art school's acceptance letter at the time, George ignored the school's expert assessment of his talent as well as any consideration of pursuing a career other than the one toward which his father directed him. But one of the dangers of relying exclusively on your Earned Wisdom is that it may be incomplete. We all have gaps in our personal wisdom: knowledge we haven't grasped, experiences we haven't tasted. George had not yet had the chance to test his talent and passion in the crucible of art school or to learn from other artists how to make a living at it. Some artists must figure out how to support themselves and their families, obviously, or we would have very few of them—but George lacked experience in that area. Because Earned Wisdom pertains only to us as individuals, it excludes the perspectives and expertise of others that are needed to make our wisdom complete.

Sometimes we lack confidence in our own wisdom because we know we don't completely understand it. At other times, we may be overconfident that we know everything we could possibly need to know. In reality, we are usually wearing blinders. Fear, ego, and stubbornness can prevent us from seeing how our personal wisdom tracks in the real world. Each of us has the opportunity to continue learning about and reassessing our past, examining it from a wiser and wiser perspective as time

> Sometimes we lack confidence in our own wisdom because we know we don't completely understand it.

goes on. Seeking appropriate Learned Wisdom from time to time can help perfect our Earned Wisdom. But what happens when we don't take that opportunity?

Let me share a personal story. My father was born in 1911 in a small Indiana farming community. He had what we now know as dyslexia. As a result, he did not learn to read until he was almost thirty years old. Even though he had a brilliant engineering mind, he was told he was dumb from an early age, and he wore that mental label all his life. Living through the Great Depression and suffering a number of personal and business setbacks gradually added to his negative outlook. As he grew older, he became a fearful, suspicious person who was obsessed with various conspiracy theories. He stayed focused on the worst case.

Upon his death at age eighty-eight, we found most of his life savings buried in his backyard flowerbeds: gold and silver coins hidden in heavy plastic tubes. I had several times suggested that he put some of these coins in the bank's safe-deposit box. He refused because he was convinced that the bank, or someone else, would steal all his money. The point is this: there was no way I was going to change his thinking or his actions based on that thinking. He was depending on his Earned Wisdom, his personal frame of reference based on his interpretation of the events in his life. This was the foundation upon which he made his decisions, and he was completely comfortable with it, even if it made no sense to me. It was who he was. Yet in his later years, my father's overwhelming past experiences robbed him of his joy of living.

My father was right to trust his Earned Wisdom, but he failed to allow that wisdom to grow. Because of his past, he needed help to tame the dangers he perceived, yet he refused any outside perspectives. Instead, his agenda became one of running from his fears by being defiant and prideful. He permitted his past to be out of balance and to smother his future. He denied himself the opportunity to determine whether his perceptions truly aligned with reality. If he had openly sought Learned Wisdom from others to work through his pain, he might have eventually found joy in life.

All my grandchildren have been diagnosed with the same dyslexia that my father had. Yet they are in classes and schools that specialize in helping kids with learning differences discover ways to learn and be successful. Imagine if my father had been offered that kind of opportunity. Rather than living with the label of "dumb," which he toted around all his life like a weighty backpack, he could have had the opportunity to overcome his handicap. With his brilliant mind, there is no telling what he could have accomplished if he had enjoyed access to the right kind of Learned Wisdom, the kind that could have led him from failure to success and from sorrow to joy.

That's the ultimate goal, isn't it? Joy in life. For most of us, that joy is dependent on having peace of mind—not that everything in life will go smoothly but that we know we're headed in the right direction and have enough resources to help us arrive. Fusing the Learned Wisdom of others into our own Earned Wisdom is a great step in overcoming life's obstacles. I believe it is the basic step to envisioning an exciting future that will outweigh our past. It is a critical component to defining your own Encore Curve.

You, like George, may be finding some obstacles that prevent you from envisioning your Encore Curve. There's a give and take here: George needs to seek more Learned Wisdom to expand his perspective and his options for the future. The more Learned Wisdom he discovers, the more of his Earned Wisdom he will understand. The more of his Earned Wisdom he understands, the more Learned Wisdom he will discover, and so on. As you read the next chapter, pay attention to how George explores both kinds of wisdom. Consider, too, what sources you need to seek out to help you envision your own exciting future.

WISDOM WORKSHEET
REVIEW YOUR PAST ▪ EMPOWER YOUR FUTURE

Throughout life you have been carrying around with you the accumulated knowledge from your experiences, both good and bad. Take off the virtual backpack and examine these experiences. What worked? What didn't work? What would you do over again? Mining the rocks of your experiences for diamonds of wisdom will direct you from the past into your future.

WHAT WORKED? *What were some of your greatest triumphs or successes?*	WHY? *Why do you consider this a success?*
1.	1.
2.	2.
3.	3.

WHAT DIDN'T WORK? *What were some of your biggest failures or regrets?*	WHY? *Why do you consider this a failure?*
1.	1.
2.	2.
3.	3.

Full-size worksheets are available at EncoreCurve.com/worksheets

WISDOM WORKSHEET
REVIEW YOUR PAST ▪ EMPOWER YOUR FUTURE

WHAT WOULD YOU DO OVER? *What would you do differently?*	WHY? *Why would you redo this experience?*
1.	1.
2.	2.
3.	3.

5

Redefine Your Past

"Age is only a number, a cipher for the records. A man can't retire his experience. He must use it."

—*Bernard Baruch, financier*

When George met Adam a few days later for their monthly lunch, Adam was unusually quiet. George broke the ice. "Adam, I appreciate your opening up about your retirement issues like you did," he said. "It means a lot to know my big brother really cares."

Adam waved off the sentiment and cleared his throat gruffly, saying, "I've been thinking a lot about that conversation. I didn't mean to scare you." He reached for his iced tea and began emptying several sugar packets into it. "Ever since we were kids trying to live up to Dad's expectations, I've felt responsible for you. I'm just worried about you and don't want you to make the same mistakes I made."

"Well, you're not responsible for me," George replied. "You're responsible only for yourself, and I'm worried about you now that you've told me about your financial situation."

Adam grimaced and looked away from George to his tea, stirring in the sugar vigorously. "Our situation's not as dire as I probably led you to believe. I was being my usual reactive self."

George figured the truth probably lay somewhere in the middle of today's statement and the one from the week before, but he kept quiet to allow his brother his dignity.

"Jennifer and I have always been impulsive with our careers and our money," Adam continued. "So I guess we all reap whatever we sow a little. But I have thought a lot about our conversation, and I've learned some things on this side of retirement that might help."

"OK, shoot. I'm learning that I need all the wisdom and experience I can gather right now."

"Well," Adam began, finishing his BLT sandwich and pushing back his plate, "there are three big ideas that I don't think most retirees are ready for. I know I certainly wasn't. First is the fact that managing your money after retirement is a lot different from managing it before you retire. When you're working and making a steady income, you can still correct mistakes. You can invest more aggressively because you have the time to make it up when you lose some of it. After retirement, you are no longer accumulating; you are spending. So you have to be a little more careful. I made the mistake of continuing to invest with my foot on the gas pedal. Then I got scared and overcorrected. You've got to be more careful on this side of retirement."

"That's where I'm lost right now," George responded. "I look at our savings and income sources, and I feel overwhelmed. I mean, how do you turn all those assets and investments into some kind of consistent income? And how much income can we expect each month? That's a big puzzle right now, but I'm hoping I can get the pieces to start fitting together pretty soon."

"George, knowing you, you'll get it figured out. But that's my second thought: get help from someone who knows what they're doing. Don't try to learn as you go. You'll regret it," Adam replied. "I wish I had asked for help from a professional, like a financial planner. I thought I knew it all, but it was a whole new experience for me. If I had sought out some direction from someone who had been through this and knew what to expect, it would have given me some peace of mind—and maybe protected our money, too."

George nodded, smiling. "'Then you will know which way to go, since you have never been this way before.'"

"Yeah, that's exactly what I needed. Where did that come from?"

"It's a verse from the Old Testament, the book of Joshua. My pastor is fond of quoting it."

"Well," Adam said, "it's great advice. Of course, you have to be wise enough to realize that retirement doesn't just change the landscape. It alters the rules of the game." He called for the check.

"And the rules right now say I'm picking up this tab," George said.

Adam's cheek twitched. George was glad they were no longer twelve and sixteen, or he might have gotten wrestled to the ground. As it was, Adam merely threw his hands up in resignation.

"Anyway," Adam said, "the third big thought I had was this: know what you are going to do. When I was working, I felt like I was somebody. Being the head of a major rep firm was a larger and more vital portion of my identity than I realized. As soon as I left, I felt like I went from being somebody important to being nobody. I suddenly had no identity. Then I went through a period of almost grief. It was like I had lost something or someone important. So my biggest advice is to make sure you are retiring to something you want to do and not just retiring from something you don't like."

"That's the problem right now," George said. "I really like what I do. I don't have a clue what I would do if I quit. Linda and Dave seem to think there is some kind of great calling out there for me to pursue. I like the way that sounds, and I know I should be thinking bigger, but I'm still not sure of the direction."

"I thought that would be somewhat of a no-brainer for you, George. What happened to all those tools stocking your garage workshop? You were always good working with your hands."

"I like to dabble, that's true, but what in the world would I make?" George said. "Linda can only use so many bookshelves."

"Your boundaries are pretty narrow there. Surely someone besides Linda needs bookshelves?"

George felt for an instant as though someone had just shaken his brain awake. "I guess I hadn't considered that anyone else would be interested in something I built," he said as they stood up to leave. "I'm not sure that's quite what I have a passion for, but it's definitely an intriguing thought."

***

The next morning, George entered the office building and headed up to Human Resources on the second floor. When the receptionist went to announce his arrival, he took one of the candies from the dish on the reception desk, slipped the wrapper off, and popped the candy in his dry mouth. Kim Thurston, head of HR, had come to the company from Mammoth a few years after he did, and he had grown to know her fairly well over the years. He double-checked the game plan that he had noted on his phone: *Health insurance. 401(k) logistics and amount.* How hard could this be to figure out?

The receptionist returned and ushered him to Kim's office for his appointment. Even though the official retirement offer hadn't been made public yet, rumors were swirling. He assumed Kim would have an idea of who was most likely to be on the short list.

The thought that he might officially find out his career was concluding gave his stomach a lurch as he opened the door to her office.

Kim seemed to read his mind as she greeted him with a smile. "Worldwide Engineering hasn't finalized the restructuring plan, so no personnel decisions have been made yet. So if you're trying to worm that out of me, George . . ." she said, sitting back at her desk and offering him a small club chair opposite, ". . . good luck! My knowledge bank on that front is empty."

He chuckled as he sat down. "The thought did occur to me."

"To you and every employee over fifty-five," she said, grimacing. She slid her readers back onto her nose, pulled his file from a neat stack on the corner of her desk, and opened it in front of her computer monitor. "Now, what questions do you have that I can answer?"

George glanced again at the list on his phone. "Well," he stammered, forgetting just how he had planned to ask the question, "the variables in retirement planning seem to be endless. I'm trying to get a big-picture view of what the options will be—how health insurance will work if I retire before I'm eligible for Medicare, maybe any changes the management will be making to 401(k) matching for retirees, and how all that works." He shifted his weight in the chair. "If I could just nail down some numbers to help me plan, I think I would be more comfortable waiting out the decision."

"Here's what I can tell you. First, Worldwide has already said they will extend health insurance benefits to the age of sixty-five for anyone taking early retirement. That's been their standard policy, and it provides a bridge to Medicare."

As Kim continued to give an overview of how the various employee benefits would work in the event of a possible change in his employment status, George realized that he knew most of that information already. "So do you have a way of projecting what the new company might offer in way of early retirement buyouts over and above our current benefits?" he asked hopefully.

"Not at this point, George. As I said when you came in, I haven't been privy to their discussions yet. I know everyone is jumpy and anxious about this. And I know they are trying to come to some solid plans as soon as possible. Frankly, I think sending out that e-mail may have caused as much harm as it was supposed to help, but that's what they decided to do. We'll just have to wait and see."

After verifying his 401(k) balances, George got up to leave.

Kim stopped him before he got to the door. "George, wait a minute. How long did you work at Mammoth before you came over here?"

"Just over thirteen years," George replied. "Why?"

"One of my projects the year before I left Mammoth and came here was to transition their old pension plan to a 401(k). Most companies have done that because providing guaranteed lifetime benefits got so expensive. My point is, when we made the change there, we grandfathered in anyone like you who had qualified for benefits but had left the company. Thirteen years should have qualified you."

George sat back down. "Now that you mention it, I do remember getting some information about it. I was young back then and didn't give it a lot of thought. Do you think it could be significant?"

"It absolutely could be very significant. As I remember, that old plan provided a lifetime retirement benefit of 2 percent of your final year's salary for every year that you worked there, and it vested after ten years. Do you remember what you were making when you left?"

"I would guess around $50,000 per year," George replied.

Kim reached for her calculator and started punching numbers as she continued, "That means that you may have an annual retirement benefit of 2 percent of $50,000 times thirteen years, or—"

"Over $13,000 per year," George said. "Wow, that is a big deal. And I wasn't even aware of it."

Kim laughed at George's quick calculation. "Don't get ahead of yourself yet. You need to contact their HR department, and they will probably have you call the plan administrator to find out the real numbers. My old boss runs that department now. Let me give you his name and phone number. In fact, I haven't talked to him lately, so let me give him a call and tell him you're going to contact him. If you mention my name, I'm sure he will help you get the right information."

This day is looking up, George thought. He tapped his fingers on his knee as he made some further mental calculations. "I can't tell you how much I appreciate your time and input, Kim. You have been a big help even if you can't give me any inside information."

"I'm glad to help, George."

"Robert has asked to meet with me this afternoon, too, to discuss my projects. Hopefully I can get his feel for where we stand. That information and our discussion should give me a much clearer picture of what retirement would look like at this point."

"Good." Kim closed his file. "I know this is a stressful time for all of us, so we have to stick together. Let me know what you find out at Mammoth."

***

After lunch, George's boss—Robert Nelson, the senior vice president in charge of engineering—called to let George know he was ready to see him in his office. George and Robert had worked together for many years and had become good friends. George appreciated Robert's ability to handle all the administrative and management responsibilities that George hated, and Robert relied on George's unique design talents and insights. Together, they made a good team.

George's earlier relief quickly tightened back into anxiety, however, as Robert explained that, over the previous few weeks, Worldwide's management had been reviewing a number of development projects that George had been working on to determine whether they should continue.

"Are they really familiar enough with the ongoing projects to see their value?" George asked.

Robert leaned back, touching his fingers together in front of his chest. He was obviously chewing on his answer. "I think I have to say not, 'Yes and no,' but, 'Yes and . . . we're getting there.' One of the issues we are working on with the new owners," he continued, "is which of our current projects fit into their corporate strategic plan. I've been traveling back and forth to their home office, helping them review those."

"I'd noticed you'd been traveling a lot," George said. "At least it's encouraging to know they're making that effort."

Robert rubbed his hand over his eyes and face, clearly weary. "Yes, although I'm sure my wife is ready for me to stay home for a while. Listen—the new corporate guys are aware of all the implications. They're doing their best to come to some conclusions. Of course, this process has a direct impact on you, George, so I'm doing all I can to speed it along. Unfortunately, since you have spent most of your time lately working specifically on everything they are reviewing, if they don't continue the projects, then early retirement may be the choice you want."

George drummed his fingers on the chair arm. He knew his boss would shoot straight with him. "Do they have a hard date for making these decisions? Will I know before the buyout deadline?" George could tell by Robert's hesitation that the answer was less favorable than he hoped. "I see. Everyone probably has to shoot in the dark a bit here."

"It's not the way I wanted to see it go down, George. You're a good friend and a valuable leader here." He tapped open the calendar on his phone and scrolled forward to the next month. "Do we even know the early-retirement deadline? As I understand, that's all still up in the air."

"Yep. Up in the air and floating around, just like the deal itself. I'm just trying to get ahead of this thing before I have to make some quick decisions."

"Understood," Robert said. He sat up straighter and rolled his chair back under his desk. "Well, I can't do anything about what they will offer companywide for those retiring early. What I can do is lobby to keep some of the important projects you are working on." He entered a few keystrokes on his laptop, clicked open a spreadsheet, and turned the screen so George could see. "There are several projects that I believe are vital to the future success of the merger—and, coincidently, have a direct impact on your future. I see part of my job as convincing Worldwide's management guys that these projects fit their corporate strategy and are worth continuing to pursue. For this, I need your help."

"Great," George replied. "Anything to move this ball down the field and help us all get clear about our futures."

Robert and George began to review each of the development projects, defining what details Robert would need on each to make his case. As they talked, George could see that some of the projects were not going to make the cut, but they also decided that some, like the Murphy project, deserved an extra push.

After two hours, they had laid out a plan, and George had a clear-cut idea of what he needed to do over the next two weeks to prepare for the meetings. As he left Robert's office, he found himself looking forward to the added work, knowing that the activity would help relieve the stress he was feeling. He also felt good about working on something that could have a direct impact on his future.

For the next few nights, George and Linda sat at the kitchen table and worked together on the worksheets Dave had given them. They listed their gifts and passions. They brainstormed about what kind of difference they wanted to make in the world around them. Each night, George watched Linda write whole paragraphs while his pen struggled to ink out even a few sentences and lists. He wanted to find the same sense of his own wisdom that she had—that self-knowledge that would give him purpose and satisfaction in his next years—but he wasn't sure how to find it.

I like to think outside the box, he wrote on Thursday evening. Then he laughed at the irony.

"What's so funny?" Linda asked. She had already finished her worksheet and was at the counter, chopping onions for some casseroles for her mom.

"I am, apparently," he said. "I get a kick out of being creative at work and putting down on paper something that didn't really exist until I thought it up. I solve difficult engineering problems that others struggle with." He held up his paper so she could see its bright white near-emptiness. "But I still can't seem to write down anything that really makes sense and energizes me about the future."

She wiped her hands on a towel and came over to the table to see what George had written. "You do like to think outside the box in many situations," she said after reading his few scrawls. "Maybe that's part of the problem. I like doing everyday things. You need a solution that's a little more out of the ordinary. It's been a long time since you inventoried your interests outside of work, and maybe you haven't set your sights high enough yet for anything to grab your attention."

"I guess that could be true. I've been trying to think of activities that fit into a slow, retired lifestyle. Maybe I'm not ready to putter around just yet."

"What I heard you say a minute ago is that you find some of your significance in doing things that others find difficult—in solving problems, in closing the gaps between what people want to do and what they can do. Didn't you do that for Dave on the building project? He sure relied on your ability to see the design in your mind as they moved forward."

George rubbed his chin. "I suppose I did do that."

"See? You didn't even have to think about what you were accomplishing for him because you enjoy it and it flows naturally from you. I, on the other hand—as you well know—wouldn't know what walls to keep or which ones to pull down. No need to smirk, George Morris. But I naturally gravitate toward wanting to make life easier and more comfortable for others. Doing simple tasks for someone, or spending time with them and listening to them, makes me feel good, like I'm doing something important. You care about that sort of thing, but it's not your first thought. So maybe you need to consider something that gives you the opportunity to solve engineering problems in unique ways. Stop thinking about what you can't do, and dream about what could be possible."

George slipped an arm around Linda's waist and gave her a gentle squeeze. "I gotta tell you, I'm a little jealous that you seem to have a clear focus while I feel so clueless."

"We'll get all this figured out," she said. "You know, I've been thinking—it really hasn't been that long since people started having the choice to do what they wanted. Only a few decades ago, the idea of retiring and choosing your future was a foreign concept to most people. They were too involved in merely surviving. They died a lot earlier than people in our generation, and they didn't have the resources to give themselves choices. I think we are pretty blessed to even have these problems to work through."

"So I'm blessed to have choices to worry about," George repeated. "Yeah, you're right. That's a great perspective." He winked at her. "Guess I'll keep working at figuring out my blessing, then."

***

On Saturday, the weather pulled them outside. Most of the city must have turned up downtown for the art show. But George didn't mind that Linda had persuaded him to go with her. He was having fun. Live jazz floated overhead among the spring buds on the trees. People young and old walked together, talking, laughing, and pointing out novelties, and the smell of funnel cakes drew him toward the food truck at the end of the block.

"Lin, I think I know where I'm headed," he said.

Linda squeezed his hand. "Have you figured out your passion, then?"

"Yep," he said. "Funnel cakes."

She swatted him playfully on the shoulder, "Oh, you and your stomach!"

"What?" he teased. "Did you think I would miraculously know what I want to do with myself after retirement just because we're surrounded by art?"

"Maybe I hoped a little," she said.

He winked at her and developed a knowing grin. "I had a feeling that was why you pushed so hard to come today. Listen, I need a break from all this stressful future planning. Let's just enjoy ourselves, huh?"

She nodded. "Fine by me."

"Good. First stop—funnel cakes."

Laughing, she let him steer her toward the food truck. They continued walking and browsing the booths as they ate. On the left, old wagon wheels rested against tables full of decorative globes of various sizes fashioned out of rusty metal strips. On the right, feathered earrings filled a display next to photographs of sleeping babies curled up with little animals—certainly not George's taste. They walked on.

On the next block, a large painting of the George Washington Bridge caught his eye. The artist had contrasted the hard, manmade structure with the soft surface of the Hudson River and the wispy clouds that faded into mist on the painting's horizon. Studying the precisely knifed lines of the crisscrossed steel archway and the thick, curved cables, George missed the beginning of Linda's question.

". . . those swirled bowls?"

"I'm sorry, Lin. What did you say?"

She pointed at a table stacked with pottery. "I wanted to know if you thought Susan would like those swirled ceramic bowls. Her birthday is next month."

"They're nice," he said. "Are they dishwasher safe? You know Susan."

"I'll go ask." She went over to the artist and waited her turn to ask her questions.

George wandered down the street a few steps, plotting where they would browse next. Up the road a bit, he saw a booth with what looked like architectural salvage pieces. As he got closer, he discovered that the artist had taken the salvage pieces and created found-object art, combining and repurposing old newel posts, business signage, and metal fan blades into abstract sculptures.

George stepped back as a strange feeling flowed through him. He looked back down the street from where he had come. The bridge . . . The wagon wheels . . . The sculptures . . . An idea began to form.

He heard Linda laughing again over his shoulder. "What is that thing?" she asked him.

He turned. "Just a yard sculpture," he said. "Part junk, part sculpture. What? You don't like it?"

"You've got that gleam in your eye," she said as her hand traveled to her hip. "You're not getting any bright ideas, are you? I'm not sure I'd want to wake up and find that thing in my living room."

He shrugged. "Just waiting for you," he said. "What did they say?"

She raised her other arm, which held a heavy-duty shopping bag. "Washable. I bought a set of four."

"Well, the trip's been a success, then."

"Has it?"

He took the shopping bag from her and clasped her fingers in his. "In my book, I think it has."

She raised an eyebrow but let her question slide off without asking it. "Ready to head back, then?" she asked instead.

"If we circle around this way, I think we'll end up close to where we parked."

As they strolled past the remainder of the art, Linda chatted happily about Susan's birthday and their granddaughter's new skills of rolling over and taking off her socks. She went on to describe how a scared little girl whose mother had been wrangling twin toddlers had latched on to Linda's offered hand at the free clinic the day before and wouldn't let go throughout the entire visit and vaccination. George heard about every third word. His head was spinning with ideas and designs and a budding plan for the future. He could feel his face slip upward into a sheepish smile. Doggone that Linda. It was a good thing she rarely gloated about being right.

Sunday afternoon, he visited the thrift store and the scrapyard. Then, every night for the next week, he spent hours in his workshop tinkering away and drawing sketches of what he planned to build. He wouldn't let Linda see any of it until he had several sketches complete.

When he showed her the sketches, he brought her out to the workshop so he could also show her the parts and pieces he would use to create some one-of-a-kind art clocks. He had found a small, round stained-glass window with an abstract pattern, and he had designed a clock in which the stained-glass disc rotated with each second. On another sketch, he had designed a large industrial clock made from a wagon wheel and an antique electric train.

"Do you think anyone would like these?"

"Like them? George, they look tremendous."

He gave her a squeeze and a wink. "Tremendous enough for the living room?"

Her eyes crinkled. "Well, maybe not the living room—but certainly somewhere with prestige."

He wasn't sure how important or significant these clocks might ever be, but allowing his creative juices to flow toward something away from the office made him feel as though someone had pumped clouds into the soles of his shoes. "I have another idea for a desktop bridge clock made with a perpetual motion machine," he said, "but I haven't figured that one out yet. I wonder what it costs to set up a booth at one of those art shows?"

"I suppose you might just have to retire so you have time to figure that out."

"It certainly makes the future seem more interesting, doesn't it?"

6

Design Your Encore GPS

*"Half our life is spent trying to find something to do with
the time we have rushed through life trying to save."*

—*Will Rogers, cowboy and columnist*

George has started making a huge breakthrough in the way he looks
at retirement. As he begins to understand his passions alongside his
skills and talents, he has started to see the future in terms of expand-
ed possibilities rather than a diminished usefulness.

You may have already found that, as a retiree, traditional thinking can be both exciting and demotivating at the same time. The
danger is letting the third stage of the Personal Progress Curve—the
Decline Stage—become our pattern for living. When we retire, we
may have a tendency to check out of productive life. Remember our
popular definition of retirement—"to be taken out of production"?
The peril of this pattern in our society is that we begin to feel as
though we are becoming irrelevant. The tangible concern of having
money issues in retirement might seem more important than the
problem of outliving your significance, but both sides of the coin
matter equally.

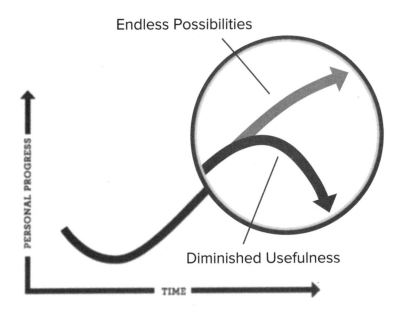

For many people, the combination of the Decline Stage, the health challenges of aging, and the fear of losing significance wedges them into a "no longer useful" thought pattern. When this happens, they start to become more preoccupied with the past and increasingly fail to plan for the future. The irony of this thinking is that when people convince themselves that they are no longer useful, this belief quickly translates into a diminished future. This thinking only accelerates with age, so the sooner you can get a grip on it, the better off you will be.

If you'll remember, I said in chapter 2 that we would be going through a three-step process—review, repackage, and repurpose. So far, you have spent some time reviewing your life history to discover your unique wisdom—that is, the experiences, lessons, triumphs, and failures that have come together to make you the unique person you are today. That's the first step. By now, you have a clearer picture of what has driven you, what you have learned, what you want to see repeated in your life, and what you want to avoid.

Although we have been reviewing our past experiences, I hope you don't stay rooted in the past. In this chapter, we are going to work on repackaging this information so it can become more useful to you. I want to show you how to take all this feedback and begin to organize it into usable wisdom that you can then apply to planning your future.

Building Your Encore Curve GPS

When George first met with Dave, the pastor quoted an Old Testament passage from the book of Joshua: "Then you will know which way to go, since you have never been this way before."[5] This idea forms a mini theme for us as we move forward into the new territory of retirement. Most of us have never been here before; we're not sure what to expect, and we don't want to make any mistakes. This leads us to the second part of our three-step process: repackaging. We now want to take all the personal wisdom pieces we've discovered and repackage or reassemble them into a system that will lead us into our future. We want to develop a GPS tracker for retirement that will help us navigate from the known to the unknown and show us how to get from where we are to where we want to be.

The GPS, which stands for Global Positioning System, has become an essential tool for most of us who travel. It is now built into the navigation system of most new cars and is

So if you can clearly define what your greatest strengths are, what you are most passionate about, and what values are most important to you, then you have the raw materials to lead you into your Encore Curve future.

available as an app for smartphones. All you have to do is input your desired destination, and the GPS will show you several route options to take you there. In a similar manner, a GPS that triangulates wisdom is the perfect tool to help us fulfill our Joshua quote. Use your GPS, and you will certainly know which way to go when you've never been this way before.

Now we are going to consolidate and organize all this thinking about your personal wisdom and build a personal GPS Profile to help you navigate the Encore Curve. In our case, the GPS stands for Giftedness, Passion, and Standards. Each of these three coordinates of your GPS system is vital. They define the energy that will lead you forward and give you an exciting vision of your future. Your Giftedness coordinate tells how you maximize your encore, your Passion coordinate tells where, and your Standards coordinate tells you why.

HOW do you operate at your best?
GIFTEDNESS

WHERE do you want to direct your energy?
PASSION

WHY does it matter what you do?
STANDARDS

Think of these three coordinates as the interconnecting circles in the following diagram. The area where they intersect represents the heart of your encore—your definition of maximum joy and significance. So if you can clearly define what your greatest strengths are, what you are most passionate about, and what values are most important to you, then you have the raw materials to lead you into your Encore Curve future.

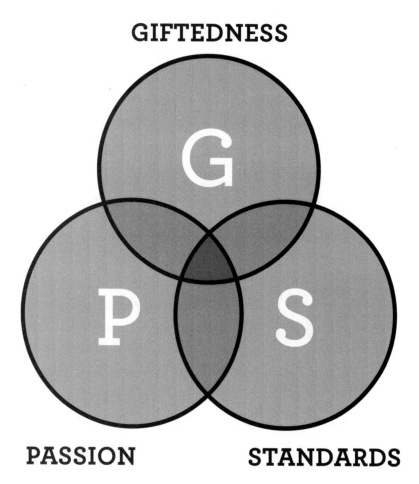

GIFTEDNESS

PASSION   **STANDARDS**

The following five exercises will help clarify your unique GPS Profile. Each coordinate is explained one at a time and followed by one or more exercises. Feel free to read through this entire chapter first before exploring the worksheets at the end—this will let you digest the material before jumping in. You can also complete each exercise as you read to the end of each section, according to your preference. Whenever you choose to work on the worksheets, though, try to write down the requested answers as quickly as you can. Don't try to edit your answers; just do a brain dump for about five to ten minutes and put some responses down on paper. You can clean it all up later, but the creative juices really flow best when you just let it happen and write down what comes to mind.

Remember to visit EncoreCurve.com/worksheets for printable worksheets and additional help. You will find five condensed GPS Profile worksheets at the end of this chapter.

Giftedness: How Do You Operate at Your Best?

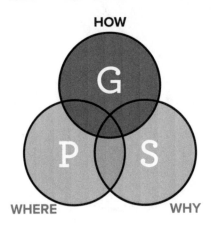

The first coordinate that will help you discover your new direction is Giftedness. Most of us have been told that we have certain weaknesses and areas we need to improve in. I can still hear my father telling me I wasn't very good at something and that I needed to practice until I was. Here's the secret that I finally learned: We all have strengths and weaknesses. If we spend all our time practicing our weaknesses, we will end up with pretty good weaknesses—but they will still be weaknesses. The best way to improve our performance and satisfaction levels is to discover what we are really good at and spend our time doing that.

That concept sounds simple enough, but it goes against what most of us have been taught. In the groundbreaking book *Now, Discover Your Strengths*, Marcus Buckingham and Donald Clifton explained Gallup Organization research that formed the background for the Clifton StrengthsFinder® assessment. Gallup discovered that, globally, "only 20 percent of employees working in the large organizations" they surveyed felt that "their strengths are in play every day."[6] The authors concluded that most corporations and organizations are built on two flawed assumptions:

1. People can learn to be competent in almost anything.
2. Peoples' potential for greater growth lies in improving their weaknesses.[7]

This conclusion implies that up to 80 percent of people in corporate America have spent their whole careers being forced to operate outside their areas of natural giftedness. Nothing seems sadder than spending your life doing things you don't like or can't do well. Having an Encore Curve future means realizing that you were built for something better. Imagine spending most of your time doing the things you are uniquely gifted at and love doing. It would be like walking on those moving sidewalks at the airport: you move faster with less effort.

Based on years of research by the Gallup Organization, Buckingham and Clifton found that each person has a unique set of strengths and that these strengths are what empower us to succeed. Your greatest possibility for future growth is based on using these strengths—not on improving your weaknesses.

Defining strength as "consistent near-perfect performance in an activity," they identified three important principles for living a strong life:

1. For an activity to be a strength, you must be able to do it consistently. It must be a predictable part of your performance, and it must give you energy, not drain energy.

2. You do not need to have a strength in every aspect of your role in order to succeed. In fact, excellent performers are rarely well rounded. They are just extraordinary in their areas of strength.

3. You can excel only by maximizing your strengths and never by fixing your weaknesses. You cannot ignore your weaknesses, but you must learn ways to manage around them.[8]

The idea of capitalizing on strengths and managing around weaknesses is easy to accept but more difficult to put into practice. Planning your Encore Curve future is the perfect time to learn how to refocus on what you do best. The stakes for your satisfaction and enjoyment levels are high. Consider this Gallup research: The people who "focus on their strengths every day . . . are more than three times as likely to say they have an excellent quality of life."[9]

Reset how you think about what you want to do during your retirement. Will it engage your strengths on a regular basis? Understanding your areas of giftedness and incompetence is critical as you plan your exciting Encore Curve future.

Discovering Your Gifts

A lot of tests exist to help you discover your strengths and how to apply them. Here is a quick exercise that will help sort these out. Think of your lifetime activities—all those things that you do routinely—as falling into one of four quadrants: Incompetent, Competent, Excellent, and Gifted.

Gifted activities are marked by these traits:

- Uniqueness—the level or manner of your performance is unique or rare

- Improvement—the activity shows continued growth and expertise
- Energy—the activity produces energy and feels "in the zone"
- Passion—you have a genuine passion for this activity and could continue forever

Excellent activities are marked by these traits:
- Excitement—the activity is stimulating and creates energy
- Superior Skill—you are more skilled than most people
- Teamwork—others want to work with you on this activity
- No Passion—you feel somewhat gifted, but you lack passion for the activity

Competent activities are marked by these traits:
- Competition—you rarely improve above minimum standards for this activity
- Anxiety—the activity creates constant worry about not performing well
- Repetition—the activity seems monotonous and draining
- Boredom—you lack enthusiasm for the activity and see no growth potential

Incompetent activities are marked by these traits:
- Frustration—progress in the activity is difficult and seems not to work
- Stress—the activity produces a high degree of tension and quick fatigue
- Failure—you frequently fail or underperform at this activity
- Confusion—you easily lose focus on the activity

For this exercise, you will list some of your lifetime activities in the appropriate box, identified as one of these four categories, on the Giftedness worksheet. Before you leap to the worksheet, however, here are some tips to make this time productive.

You will note that this exercise requires you to admit that you are incompetent at doing certain things. This may be a shocking idea, as the world has always told us that we need to excel in everything, but admitting incompetence in certain things is often the first step in focusing on your strengths and finding a more fulfilling life.

As you do this exercise, think of all the activities below the line—Incompetent and Competent—as ones that tend to drain your energy and that need to be avoided or minimized if possible. On the other hand, all the activities above the line—Excellent and Gifted—tend to increase your energy when you do them. What would life be like if you could spend 80 percent of the rest of your days doing the above-the-line activities?

Start with the Incompetent list first. These activities should be the easiest to identify, while the Gifted section may be the hardest. Don't try to make an exhaustive list at first. Just jot down three or four things as quickly as you think of them; then set the exercise aside and come back to it during the week.

Finally, remember how Linda observed George's ability to see certain design elements even when he wasn't really trying to do so? As she noted, this ability just flowed out of who he was. This illustrates the kind of giftedness we all possess in some way. It also demonstrates how someone else may see things we do not or cannot see on our own. So if you are serious about this, let someone else (like a spouse or a close friend) fill in the sheet based on his or her observations of you. You can even send a note to several friends asking them what they think your unique ability or giftedness is.

Passion: Where Do You Want to Direct Your Energy?

Passion is the second coordinate of our GPS system. Passion has to do with love. It asks the questions "What do you love doing?" and "Whom do you love?" If Giftedness is the coordinate that tells you the "how" (the mode by which you will maximize your Encore potential) then Passion is the

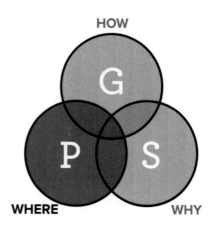

"where" (the direction and areas to apply your giftedness so you can find maximum joy). For our purposes, we'll divide Passion into two branches: action and impact. We want to discover what actions to take (what you love doing) and whom you want those actions to impact (people or organizations you love).

Action: What Do You Love Doing?

Benjamin Disraeli, a nineteenth-century British prime minister, once said, "Man is only great when he acts from passion." Widespread reporting indicates that at least 75 percent of the population does not know what their true passion is. In other words, we don't know what we really like and dislike. George encountered this difficulty. What about you?

For most of us, life has been a blur of busyness with an occasional week or so of vacation thrown in to break the routine. Now, as retirement approaches, you are facing vacation every day. That may sound like a slice of heaven, but you run the risk of letting time turn into another blur of random activity without much to show for it. This is where passion comes in. Passion drives happiness and fulfillment. Passion helps you define what is uniquely important to you. Doing what you love will give you a big push toward a satisfying and fulfilling life. In fact, a good definition of retirement is paying yourself to do what you love.

You can find many online tests and questionnaires that can help you discover your passion. But for our purposes now, in this first Passion exercise, I want you to make some lists in answer to questions that take you from the past through the present and into the future:

- What did you love doing as a child?
- When does time fly by for you?
- What will you regret not doing or trying?

Consider the following important ideas as you answer.

Past: What Did You Love Doing as a Child?

Our passions often stem from something we discovered when we were young. Giving weight to the things you loved as a child is probably the simplest way to unearth what pursuits hold the potential to light up your days. When we were kids, before the grown-ups affected us with their ideas, most of us knew exactly who we were and what made us happiest. For instance, were you obsessed with horses or other animals? Did you love painting or drawing? Did you sing at the top of your lungs until people begged you to stop?

Like George, a friend of mine had always enjoyed drawing, but he never had time to pursue it. When he retired at age sixty-two, he began taking art lessons, and today he is one of the most in-demand watercolor artists in the area. He began painting special scenes for people on request. For instance, he used an old photograph to paint my wife's grandfather's old house, where her family was raised and had gathered for holidays. He painted a number of scenes depicting special events at his church. He found a way to focus his passion and make a lasting impact on other people. So consider: what did you love doing as a child?

Present: When Does Time Fly By for You?

We all know how time seems to drag when we're doing something that we can't stand or find boring. For instance, a friend of mine who's a physician reports that when he sees a long line of sore throats and scraped knees, he watches the clock constantly and can't wait until he is done. However, when a patient comes in who is depressed, anxious, or newly diagnosed with a condition that would benefit from an altered lifestyle, this doctor suddenly comes alive as he counsels that patient. Not surprisingly, this doctor's true passion is life and health coaching, which often involves spending larger chunks of time teaching and encouraging patients than swabbing throats does. So what do you do that makes time seem to fly by? What would you love to spend hours doing that you never have enough time for? That's a passion, and you probably need to do it more than you are.

Future: What Will You Regret Not Doing or Trying?

We all have regrets. When you reexamined your past in the previous chapters, you probably discovered that you had several. There are things we wish we had done but didn't do, and there are things we did that we shouldn't have. That's part of life. We can carry these regrets around as rocks in our backpack, or, rather than fret about what might have been, we can understand that the past is behind us and look forward to tomorrow. One way to view retirement is as an opportunity to begin living a life of no regrets. To do this, write out a list of what you might regret not having done by the end of your life. Some call this a "bucket list" because it consists of things you want to do before you kick the bucket. Dream, but be realistic about your bucket list, because we are going to combine it with the lists from other exercises to create your Encore Curve future. What will you regret not doing or trying?

Impact: Who or What Do You Love?

Our lives are lived in community, not in isolation. As we interact with others, we influence them, and they influence us. The problem is that most of us are not intentional about our impact. It's something that, for good or ill, just happens. Linda started George thinking in an "impact" direction when she reminded him of how he helped Pastor Dave solve his building problem, but he still hasn't fully embraced the importance of this element.

One dictionary definition of "impact" is the force exerted by a new idea, concept, technology, or ideology. Another way to describe it is as influence, which is often defined as the power to change or affect someone or something, as the power to cause changes without directly forcing them to happen, or as someone who affects change. Thus influence relates to the idea of using your wisdom, experience, passion, and giftedness to effect a change in another person, in groups of people, or in an organization.

When we try to think about whom we want to or could influence, many of us come up dry beyond the expected answers of "children" and "grandchildren." In fact, some of us find the very idea of impacting another person difficult. I've heard responses to this idea that range from "I mind my own business, and don't want to force my ideas onto someone else" to "If everyone thought the way I do, the world would be a better place."

Think about your life for a minute. Which has given you more meaning—what you have received or what you have given? Which has brought you a bigger feeling of significance—the things you have bought and own or the things you have done and shared? If one of a retiree's greatest fears is outliving his or her significance, can that fear be made up for by acquiring more stuff or by giving back? For most of us, meaning comes not from cutting back our contributions to society but from increasing them. As business coach Dan Sullivan observed in his Strategic Coach® program, "Most people don't die from old age but from lack of meaning and purpose. They don't die because they run out of years but because they run out of contributions to make." That's why identifying your impact is so critical. Without it, your retirement might be shorter than you'd hoped.

Let me insert a personal example of how some of these elements fit together. I have a passion for teaching Bible studies. I also enjoy—and have been told I have a distinct knack for—writing devotional thoughts. All four of Jean's and my grandchildren have now reached their teenage years, and we love them dearly. But we are beginning to lose the type of close contact we had with them when they were children. Their lives have become busy, and, as adolescents do, they tend to think they are independent freethinkers. (By age twenty-one, they will again realize how wise their parents and grandparents are, but that is a few years off.) So to maintain a semblance of influence, I have begun to write short devotional and motivational thoughts for them. I post these on a blog—a relevant format for my grandchildren. This endeavor makes use of my GPS Profile by incorporating my gift for writing, my passion for teaching and for my grandchildren, and my standard that passing wisdom down through the generations requires intentional action.

The idea I want to convey is that we all influence other people, whether we intend to or not. If we do have influence, why not become intentional about it? Why not use what you have learned and believe as a basis for making a greater, more lasting, and more positive impact on the people and organizations you care about? Think of your family members, friends, fellow employees, church or organization members, and so on. What greater gift can we give than to use all this wisdom we have accumulated over our lifetimes by sharing it in a useful way with others?

Making a Difference

My friend Chris, who has a real passion for fishing, retired several years ago. The first couple of years after retirement, he seemed to take a fishing trip every month. Sometimes he went to exotic locations, and sometimes he just went to the local lake. After a while this got old, and Chris began to look for ways he could use his love of fishing to help others. He is now actively involved in a program that takes wounded veterans on fishing expeditions as part of their recovery. It has given him a chance to share an activity he loves in a way that is making a huge difference in the lives of dozens of young men.

My wife, Jean, is another good example of someone using her gifts and passion to make a real impact. She has a heart for the homeless and for families in transition. With her degree in home economics, she has a gift for decorating and hospitality. For many years, she has spent several days a week, on a voluntary basis, setting up apartments for new families at a transition-housing ministry. These apartments are often the first real homes that these families have had and are integral in helping them get on their feet. Jean's job is hard and physically demanding, but she does it with great joy and purpose because she knows it makes a difference in peoples' lives.

In this second Passion exercise, thinking about the people who have influenced you will help you discover whom you want to influence. Consider these groups on the Impact worksheet at the end of the chapter:

- List two or three people who have made a significant impact on you and why.
- List the people, groups, and organizations that you currently influence or that you want to impact in coming years. Be sure to write down how you want to do so.

This second list could include activities such as spending time with your grandkids by teaching them to play golf, serving on nonprofit boards that desperately need wise guidance, caring for aging parents, or teaching young children. Whatever you come up with, make sure you build the idea of giving back and sharing all the great wisdom you have accumulated over your lifetime into your retirement planning. This is not only for the sake of others but also for the sake of your own feeling of significance. Retirees may find this thought from pastor and author Chip Ingram especially poignant: "When most people finally realize that we're usually only remembered for the people we touched rather than the things we accomplished, it's almost too late to invest in much eternal treasure."[10]

Standards: Why Does It Matter What You Do?

For this third coordinate of our GPS system, we will answer the "why" question of your encore: "Why does pursuing this particular Encore Curve future matter to you and others?" This coordinate is the key factor in maximizing your sense of significance.

Your quality of life is directly related to your personal standards. A standard is a rule or expectation about the level of excellence you require in something. Personal standards form the basis for the habits that we build into our lives; therefore, how we live is a reflection

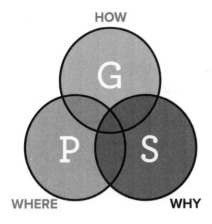

of our personal standards. Retirement is a great time to reset those standards. If we don't expect much, we won't get much.

Earlier, we discussed the dangers of slipping into the Decline Stage during retirement. One of these dangers is that we become more relaxed about our standards. As comedian Robin Williams said before his tragic suicide, "You realize you are violating your standards faster than you can lower them." When we are actively engaged in the workplace, we develop certain habits. For instance, we get up early, we go to work, we read, we interact with people, and so on. In short, we are productive and focused. Retirement has a way of changing all that. Without a focused purpose, inertia can take over, and we can find ourselves less focused and less purposeful. Ultimately, our habit patterns change, and we fall into the decline-curve mentality.

The point of building an Encore Curve is to replace this common relaxing of standards with an exciting new vision and purpose. So in this final pair of exercises for building your GPS Profile, we will look at standards from two perspectives—values and habits— by asking two key questions:

- What is important to believe?
- What is important enough to act on?

Core Values: What Is Important to Believe?

In his great hit "Strangers in the Night," Frank Sinatra sings a chorus that sounds a lot like "do, be, do, be, do." I've often thought how that chorus describes our lives. What we "do" flows out of who we "be," and who we "be" flows out of what we "do." It's kind of the chicken and the egg conundrum: Which comes first—who you are or what you do? I think it's both. That's the thing about values and beliefs: they are part of the "be" that produces our actions and habit patterns—our "do."

A person's values are about as subjective as you can get. They are very personal, yet they drive our behavior in unexpected ways. George's values are pretty clear. He cares deeply about his wife, Linda, and his family. Based on his actions so far, he seems deeply driven by faith. And he cares about engineering design. As we will see, he will begin to take actions based on how these three areas of importance come together.

To help you get a handle on this concept of value or importance, answer the following questions. Be sure to consider both parts: the "what" and the "why."

- What ideas or ideals do you value the most? Why?
- What personal relationships hold the most value for you? Why?
- Of what achievements are you most proud? Why?
- If you were to dedicate one full year to something, what might that be? Why?

Habits: What Is Important to Act On?

A small river runs behind our cabin in the mountains of northern New Mexico. To most people, it looks like a mountain stream, but it is called the Red River. It flows with water collected from melting snow and smaller, spring-fed streams high in the mountains. As the snow melts at higher altitudes, the water makes its way down in trickles, which flow into larger streams, which finally flow into the river. I've always been struck by how this process naturally repeats itself. Over the years, the water has cut deep channels, which it now follows. It has no choice. It is following the path of least resistance.

We do the same thing. We follow the path of least resistance in our lives. We call these paths "habits," and they become as natural to us as the water flowing down the mountain. According to Charles Duhigg, author of *The Power of Habit*, most habits occur in a three-step loop. First, a cue or trigger tells the brain which automatic mode or habit to follow. Then we actually follow the routine. Finally, there is a reward that helps your brain decide which loop is worth repeating. Over time, as we repeat the process, the cue, routine, and reward become automatic, and a new habit pattern is born.[11]

The Habit Hole

The problem for most retirees is what I call the Habit Hole. When we stop working, massive sets of habit patterns that we have developed around our jobs simply disappear. Our daily routine—when we get up, where we go, what we read, what we think about, and with whom we interact—suddenly changes. We no longer have the same cues, follow the same routines, or receive the same rewards as we did when we worked.

Because nature abhors a vacuum, our new Habit Hole will instantly begin to fill up with other behaviors—ones that we may find temporarily pleasing but that don't add constructively to our Encore Curve pursuits. We suddenly find a new affinity for daytime television, check Facebook incessantly, or fritter away countless hours with no mindful purpose or direction.

One client admitted to me that she had formed the habit of watching daytime news shows and stock reports for over ten hours per day. This habit had developed slowly as she recovered from surgery. Now she was addicted, and it showed in her outlook. In a period of months, she had transformed from a vivacious, socially engaged woman to a fearful, negative, and withdrawn human being. Another client retired a couple of years before his wife and got bored. His daily routine was to get up late, play with his tools in the garage until lunchtime, then head to a local dive to eat and drink beer with friends all afternoon. He described his postretirement life as having "dropped out."

There is nothing wrong with any of these activities, but they can get out of control and become part of a new routine of habits we never intended to form. If we don't take intentional action to fill our Habit Holes, we will find ourselves following new paths of least resistance, including new habit patterns that can eat away at our lives just as flowing water eats away the soil and digs a riverbed. We will suddenly find ourselves in the middle of the decline curve, not understanding how we got there. As a friend once pointed out, the only difference between a rut and a grave is the dirt in your face.

Therefore, we must take great care how we fill that Habit Hole after every major life transition. Periodic review of our habit patterns will keep us energized toward significance. Let's look at some basic facts about habits and why they have so much power in our lives. Then we will do an exercise to help focus on the types of habits we want to develop or eliminate in retirement.

- Each habit may have a cluster of others attached to it. Often, these clusters strengthen the central habit and insulate it from change. For example, if you want to form a habit of daily exercise, you may have to change the time you go to bed or get up in the morning.

- We can change only one habit at a time. In most situations, making too many changes at once is such a big shock that it will doom you to failure. Like the melting snow in the mountains, we tend to seek the path of least resistance—the easiest way. Trying to make too many changes at one time overwhelms us and invites frustration.

- It takes time to change a habit. The old rule described twenty-one days as the standard. But scientists now estimate that it can take, on average, up to sixty-six days to establish a new habit.[12] The main issue is consistency. If you repeat a new activity each day for sixty-six days, you will find that the new activity has become automatic—a new path of least resistance. That means that as early as two months into retirement, purposeless behaviors that will send you quickly down the decline curve may become set into your routine.

- The best way to change an old habit is to replace it with a new and better one. Stopping an old habit but replacing it with nothing creates a vacuum that must be filled. So as you consider new habits, think in terms of replacing unwanted behaviors with more desirable ones rather than simply trying to stop the old behaviors.

For this exercise, answer the following questions on the Standards: Habits worksheet at the end of the chapter. Remember that you can also find full-size worksheets and additional help at EncoreCurve.com/worksheets.

- As you consider retirement, what habits or routines do you anticipate will go away and create vacuums?
- What old habits would you like to eliminate? Why?
- What new habits would you like to begin? Why?
- What is the most important habit change (for yourself) you can think of? Why?

Putting All the Pieces Together

After you have finished your lists from the five exercises in this chapter exploring the basic elements of your GPS Profile—your unique Giftedness, Passion, and Standards—the next step is to construct your GPS Navigator. This Navigator will show where your three coordinates overlap. The area where these three groups intersect will give you a good reading on where and how to design your Encore Curve.

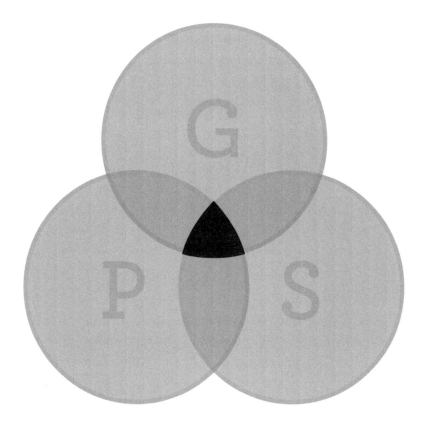

In chapter 8, we will identify a much smaller list of activities where your Giftedness, Passion, and Standards overlap. To prepare for this list, I recommend you review each of the five worksheets and circle the two or three most meaningful items on each. This final list should provide the power for designing a fulfilling rest-of-life experience.

Do you see that if you ignore any of the three areas of your GPS Profile, your ideas for the future will lack the full significance and enjoyment you desire? George has been mulling over his current plans, and while he's more engaged and enthused about retiring than ever before, he realizes that something is still missing. As he keeps looking back on his life, he knows he has some real gifts and is certainly passionate about his family, but he keeps thinking that he wants to make a bigger impact. He feels he has yet to completely solve the puzzle of what to do with his future.

Let's rejoin him and find out what answers he discovers.

GIFTEDNESS WORKSHEET
THE FOUR QUADRANTS

Quickly jot down three or four activities–things that you routinely do in your personal or business life–for each of the four quadrants. Begin with the Incompetent quadrant (#1). Admitting that some activities are difficult is the first step toward being able to focus on your strengths and creating a fulfilling life! Work your way toward the Gifted quadrant (#4).

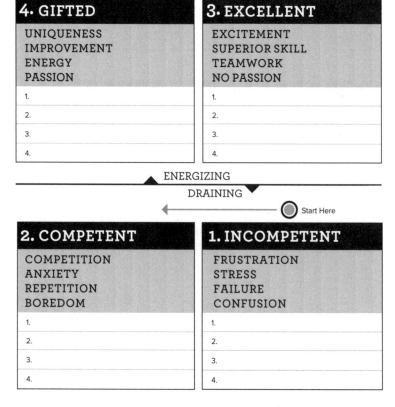

4. GIFTED	3. EXCELLENT
UNIQUENESS IMPROVEMENT ENERGY PASSION	EXCITEMENT SUPERIOR SKILL TEAMWORK NO PASSION
1.	1.
2.	2.
3.	3.
4.	4.

ENERGIZING

DRAINING

Start Here

2. COMPETENT	1. INCOMPETENT
COMPETITION ANXIETY REPETITION BOREDOM	FRUSTRATION STRESS FAILURE CONFUSION
1.	1.
2.	2.
3.	3.
4.	4.

Full-size worksheets are available at EncoreCurve.com/worksheets

PASSION WORKSHEET
DO WHAT YOU LOVE ▪ LOVE WHAT YOU DO

Passion drives happiness and fulfillment and helps
you define what is uniquely important to you.
Spend some time digging into your past and also dreaming
about your future.

PAST: *WHAT DID YOU LOVE DOING AS A CHILD?*	
1.	4.
2.	5.
3.	6.

PRESENT: *WHEN DOES TIME FLY BY FOR YOU?*	
1.	4.
2.	5.
3.	6.

FUTURE: *WHAT WILL YOU REGRET NOT HAVING DONE?*	
1.	4.
2.	5.
3.	6.

Full-size worksheets are available at EncoreCurve.com/worksheets

PASSION WORKSHEET
MAKING AN IMPACT ON OTHERS

Take some time to think about what and whom you are passionate and about how you can use these things to impact these people and organizations now and perhaps into the future.

IMPACT ON ME	
List two or three people who have made a significant impact on you and the reasons why.	
WHO	WHY
WHO	WHY
WHO	WHY

IMPACT ON OTHERS	
Who or what would you like to impact with your Encore Curve and how?	
WHO/WHAT	HOW
WHO/WHAT	HOW
WHO/WHAT	HOW
WHO/WHAT	HOW
WHO/WHAT	HOW
WHO/WHAT	HOW
WHO/WHAT	HOW

Full-size worksheets are available at EncoreCurve.com/worksheets

STANDARDS WORKSHEET
VALUES: WHAT'S IMPORTANT TO BELIEVE?

Personal standards are what build your daily habits and thus show what is important to you. Answering the questions below will tell you more about who you are and what you value.

What ideas or ideals are the most important to you? Why?

_____   _____

_____   _____

_____   _____

Which personal relationships mean the most to you? Why?

_____   _____

_____   _____

_____   _____

Of what accomplishments are you most proud? Why?

_____   _____

_____   _____

_____   _____

If you could dedicate one full year to something, what would it be? Why?

_____

_____

Full-size worksheets are available at EncoreCurve.com/worksheets

STANDARDS WORKSHEET
HABITS: SHOW WHAT YOU VALUE

What you value and how you spend your time are inextricably intertwined. Combining the insight from your values worksheet with your answers to the following questions should reveal the importance of making intentional choices for your daily activities in your Encore Curve.

As you think about your future, what habits or routines are most likely to **cease or change** and create a vacuum?

_____   _____

_____   _____

_____   _____

What **old habits** would you like to eliminate or change? Why?

_____   _____

_____   _____

_____   _____

What **new habits** would you like to begin practicing? Why?

_____   _____

_____   _____

_____   _____

What's the most important habit change that you can think of? Why?

_____

_____

_____

Full-size worksheets are available at EncoreCurve.com/worksheets

7

Find Your Encore Future

"To love what you do and feel that it matters—could anything be more fun?"

—*Katherine Graham, publisher*

Early Monday morning found George downtown, toting a bag of several large items back to the Central Square parking lot where he had left his car. As he neared Main Street, he saw Pastor Dave trying to open the post office door while balancing two large boxes. George hollered, and Dave turned his head when he heard George's voice.

"Need some help with that?" George asked.

"Thanks," Dave said. "My wife collects toys for the kids at refugee camps in Africa, and the boxes seem to get heavier every month."

George opened the door and held it for Dave, who moved through sideways with his boxes.

"Where'd you come from?" Dave asked.

George held up his bag of parts. "Collecting scraps for a new hobby."

"Does that mean you've made progress on the retirement question?"

George stepped through the door with his friend, moving out of the way of a postal customer who was leaving. "If only it were just one question," George said. "But we've made progress."

"Meaning solid numbers?" Dave asked, waiting for George to grab the handle on the door to the customer service area.

"Maybe not solid, but I can at least make out certain figures floating in the air," he said. He stepped ahead and once again swung the door wide so Dave could fit through.

The pastor sidled through and set the packages on the counter running alongside the line to the clerk's window. "So," he said, "you've gotten to floating numbers. What about the other side of the coin? Does your new hobby have anything to do with that?"

Where should he start? "It does," he said. "I've picked up an old interest in art, and I've even started designing some one-of-a-kind timepieces."

"You're building timepieces?" Dave said. "That sounds promising."

"It is. I might even try to sell some of them at local art fairs."

Dave whistled. "That's a far cry from our last conversation. I'm excited for you."

"Thanks." He smiled. "I guess retirement won't be so awful after all." The line moved forward, and George turned to go, clapping Dave on the back and saying, "I'll see you Sunday."

"George?"

George swiveled back to face his friend.

Dave was looking at him, studying. "You don't seem all that excited about this new adventure."

"No, I am," he said. "There's just still a lot to figure out."

"Lots of change, huh?" The line moved again. "No, really, George. Don't think hard—just finish this phrase: 'I'm really excited about art and clock making, but . . .'"

"But . . . I wonder if it's significant enough," he said. The words surprised him as he said them aloud.

The clerk motioned for Dave to step up to the window. "Those are important words," Dave said. "Can you hang around a moment while I mail these?"

"Of course," George said, and he waited by the door, thinking. Was he merely anxious about the upcoming changes? Or were the clocks still not the answer for him?

After a few moments, Dave rejoined him, and the two walked toward the cars in the parking lot. "You wonder if clocks are significant enough," Dave said. "Flesh that out for me."

"The clocks are fun, and fun is good. But I guess now that I've really started thinking about moving beyond my career, I'm finding that I want to do something truly meaningful, and I don't know if the clocks will fulfill that desire. It's like I've built up this lifetime of experience and expertise that should be important to someone. I can't just forget about it and leave it at the side of the road."

"OK," Dave said. "So is there a particular issue, world problem, or nagging feeling that you always wished you could do something about?"

"Of course."

"So what's stopping you?"

George chuckled. "Because it's that simple, right?"

"Not simple," Dave allowed. "But good. And fill-you-up worth it."

They arrived at George's SUV first. He chewed on Dave's statement as he opened the liftgate and put his scrapyard purchases inside. "I'm not sure what you're getting at," he said finally.

"You're asking how to find your significant impact," Dave answered.

"Decide to save the world, and it happens. Right," said George as he shut the back of his SUV and walked around to the driver's side. "I think I was asking about something on a much smaller scale."

"George, if I know anything about you, it's this: you haven't been satisfied with your own answers because you won't be satisfied with the smaller scale. Just think a minute. My wife organizes community garage sales, so sending toys to refugees flows naturally out of that. What answers to the world's problems do you already have?"

George had started to step into the car, but he stopped. He stopped grasping for ideas, too. He stopped thinking, really. He just knew. The Murphy project. Water desalination. He knew how to provide clean water to those without it. He knew how to create solar panels that could bring power to people without a reliable electric grid. He knew how to plan out and oversee a design project that would bring better technology to those who struggled with the challenges of poverty and lack of access to basic necessities. He turned and raised his eyes to Dave's, whose face acted like a mirror to his own, spreading into a wide smile.

"How did you do that?" George asked. "I've been trying to figure that out for weeks!"

Dave shrugged. "Then you will know which way to go, since you have never been this way before," he said.

George crossed his arms and leaned back against the doorframe. "All right, wise guy. If you're so smart, then where does the money come from to take engineering design to villages in need?"

Dave's eyes twinkled. "You're the problem solver. I thought that was your department."

***

After work, George couldn't wait to take another stab at filling out his worksheets and future goals. Within five minutes, he had an entire page filled. As soon as he began to write down some of the big goals, something clicked, just as it did whenever he was designing a new piece of engineering. The ideas flowed onto the page.

His first goal was to be a more engaged grandfather with his grandkids. He hadn't realized just how important they were to him and how much he could influence them. He wanted them to remember him as a positive, happy person rather than the serious, sometimes harsh man he remembered his father being.

Second, he wanted to work with Linda on her mission projects. He realized that, through their discussions lately, he had become more interested in what she was doing, and he wanted to find ways of sharing it with her. Even more, he wanted to work with her to figure out how to be involved in bringing sustainable resources to impoverished villages overseas and whom he could connect with to do so. The thought was intimidating but incredibly exciting all at the same time.

Beneath those two goals, he wrote that he wanted to reserve time for creating his art clocks—or whatever else he dreamed up and could make. He would sell them if he could, but he wanted that activity to be a respite rather than a demanding responsibility—not a job, but a way to continue learning and to grow his creativity and artistry.

And finally, he wrote down some financial and travel goals.

He had never felt so excited and so scared. So many of these ideas were new thoughts, and he didn't have a clue as to how they were going to happen. He just knew that they were important. He took his worksheet into the den, where Linda was relaxing and watching her favorite show. She paused the television and gave him her attention, reading through his list and descriptions. He could hardly wait for her to get to the bottom of the page.

"If I could do all this," he said, "my life would really mean something. I think I've finally found a good direction for me."

"I'm impressed, George. Your list makes me look forward to times ahead even more."

"Then why do you have such a worried look?"

"Do I? I guess I don't want you to be disappointed after discovering all these passions and goals inside you. I've gone over and over the budget based on your estimated income numbers, and based on what we know now, I haven't been able to balance it."

"Did you include the $13,000 a year for my Mammoth pension? I got confirmation today that I am eligible for that amount."

"I did, and I'm glad to hear that, but—George, do you realize that amount just covers the $1,000 extra we're chipping in each month to care for Mom? When are we going to hear what the company is going to offer us? I'm really getting concerned."

George thought back to what Adam had told him about having less room to correct financial mistakes after retirement. "Maybe we need to rethink how much we're spending on your mom's care," he said.

Linda looked up at him sharply. "It costs what it costs, George. What do you want me to do? Leave her alone when I can't be there?"

"No, that's not—"

"I'm sorry, George. I know you're trying to be practical. But we can't very well stay with her at night either. We'd never sleep."

George recalled Adam's recommendation to get help. He realized he was now ready to take that next step. "I'll see if I can get an update from Robert tomorrow," he said. "And I think it's time we try to find a financial planner to help us draw up a few scenarios for what we're looking at."

"I suppose that would be OK," Linda agreed. She picked up the remote and restarted her show.

"Good," George said. "Because you're right—it's great to dream of an exciting future saving the world or doing whatever new things we want, but we still have to pay for it." He leaned over, kissed the crown of her head, and left her to her much-deserved down time. As for him, he spent the next hour searching the Internet for good financial planners in his area before calling it quits and heading to bed.

***

The next day, he popped his head into Robert's office. "Got a minute?" he asked.

Robert was participating in a conference call on his laptop, but he waved George in.

George took a seat and heard the various people on the call sign off. Robert closed the program and shut his computer. His mouth was set in firm line, and his eyes seemed focused on some place in his own head rather than on George or the room. George waited for him to process his thoughts.

"Sometimes a forest gets so big that the woodcutters think every tree looks the same," Robert finally said.

"Was that the Worldwide management team?" George asked, indicating the laptop.

"Yeah," Robert said. "Committee rule." He sighed. "Change is never easy."

"No," George replied, "but sometimes it kick-starts something good right when we need it."

Robert looked up sharply. "That's an unexpected perspective coming from you right now."

"Let's just say I've learned a lot about myself in the past four weeks." He tapped his knee. "So Worldwide isn't biting on the development and design projects yet?"

Robert shook his head. "They're still sniffing around, but I'm doing a lot more fishing than catching, George. I'm afraid I may lose the battle here."

George knew that Robert's comment would have unsettled him two days ago, but today, his stomach stayed calm, and he found his disappointment manageable. "I've been thinking a lot about this, and I realized we may have been taking the wrong approach," he said. "Rather than analyzing these projects from our perspective and trying to justify them based on what we want, let's look at them from Worldwide's perspective and narrow our push to the ones that will most benefit Worldwide in the long run. What do you think?"

"Sure," Robert answered. "That's a good idea. Circle our wagons around the trees that we're most likely to be able to rescue from the woodcutters and their indiscriminate chainsaws. The question is—how will we convince them these projects are in their company's best interest? Worldwide already laid out a lot of capital for this merger."

"Maybe looking for immediate profit is the wrong strategy," George said. "Worldwide has long-term goals, right?"

"Of course."

"So let's look at it this way: In ten years, how will each of these projects have moved the department toward the overall goals of the company at that time? Maybe we can even look at some of our initial plans and modify them so that they help Worldwide move in the direction its management wants to go—especially if we can also help the company show profitability in the short run."

"That's an idea," Robert said. "How do you propose to go about that?"

"Well, take the Murphy project, for example. It's the experimental desalination product I've spent so much time on. It certainly isn't near to being profitable now, but it could become a game changer in time. Also, if Worldwide justified the investment based on the potential social impact of creating sustainable water sources around the world, they could get a lot of good press now. Every big company needs to be seen as a good citizen rather than a corporate bully."

"That's an interesting approach. From what I've learned about the new management, they just might go for that. Not all bottom line now, but huge promise for the future and some nonprofit motive today. Great idea. How do you propose we proceed?"

"What if I draw up the numbers for each project and extrapolate them five and ten years out?" George said. "Then I'll compare how much revenue, increased reputation, or other intangibles we can expect with the expenditures and required personnel hours over the same period. If we can find which projects are the most profitable and self-sustaining in terms of Worldwide's goals, maybe they'll bite."

"I like that," Robert said. "Get Worldwide looking further into the future and force them to see how the projects will become more asset than liability."

"And maybe we'll see better, too, why some of the projects don't fit their goals."

"It certainly can't hurt," Robert said. "What gave you the idea to look backward from the future?"

"It's these worksheets I've been using to get a handle on my own future plans. It really helps to consider where you want to be in a set amount of time so you can determine what preparation steps that would require in the meantime. Sometimes you see that a goal or a time frame needs to change, or maybe you realize that you need to reprioritize your current activities to reach the goal in the amount of time you want."

Robert shook his head again, but this time he was smiling. "There are a lot of people in management who could use that kind of wisdom."

"Sometimes change kick-starts something good," George repeated.

"I see that. So, speaking of your future, that's all going better, then?"

"It's not bad, actually. In terms of what I want to do if I retire, I'm starting to see how my future could be even better than now. But I really need to get a handle on the financial side, regardless of what early retirement deals are cooking. I gathered a long list of financial planners from the Internet last night, and I have no idea how I'm going to evaluate them all or choose between them. So I've kind of thrown myself back onto the clueless side of the ledger, just when I was getting the life-goal side looking promising."

"Oh, I can help you there," Robert said. "First of all, make sure it's someone who charges a fee for their advice and will work with you to build a solid long-term plan. You don't want someone who merely sells investment products on a commission basis—I made that mistake starting out. I got advice, but I didn't receive the kind of in-depth planning I was really looking for." He swiped open the contacts list on his phone and began scrolling through it. "If you want, I can give you the name of the guy I use. He's a real straight shooter, and I think you'd like him."

George had his pen ready. "Sounds great. What's his name?"

"Mike Hartsfield. I've worked with him for several years now, and I couldn't be happier. I think his experience and partnership will be one of the most valuable assets I take into retirement one day."

George whistled. "That's a solid recommendation if I ever heard one," he said as he finished writing down the information. "I'll look into it."

"George, thanks for your insights today," Robert said. "Start pulling up some of those numbers, and I'll get help writing up the new report."

"Will do," George said.

8

Make Your Future Bigger Than Your Past

"You got to be careful if you don't know where you're going, because you might not get there."

—*Yogi Berra, baseball manager*

George has just made a big jump. With Dave's help, he was able to visualize something he had never seen before. He saw himself using his gifts and expertise to help people on a larger scale than he had ever before imagined possible. At the same time, George's new outlook also allowed him to be bolder in solving the business problems facing the company. To reach this point, George had to envision himself outside of his comfort zone and be able to think bigger thoughts.

Let me tell you what I mean. We recently returned from a trip to England and Scotland. In Scotland, we toured several castles built hundreds of years ago. Most of these castles perched on top of hills or stood solidly in the middle of moats to protect the occupants from invading armies. Over the years, the inhabitants added extra protections such as cannons, armories, and reinforced walls to further defend themselves—and the status quo.

As I walked through one of these strongholds, I thought about how most of us live in our own "castles" to protect ourselves from invasions. We settle into a comfort zone. When we feel threatened by the dangers and pain of change, we add thicker walls and defenses. The more time we spend in our castles, the more comfortable we become. We grow used to our surroundings. We adapt to living with only what we have available in our safe spaces. The longer we stay inside, resisting significant changes, the thicker we build the walls, and the harder it becomes to venture outside.

Even though many have spent a lifetime building up these walls, they will inevitably crumble, and the outside will force its way in. Life is about change, not maintaining the status quo, regardless of how hard we resist. The thicker we build our walls, the more painful it will be when they crumble.

But here's the thing: almost all personal growth takes place outside of the comfort zone. Sometimes we are forced out; sometimes we choose to step outside. The threat of early retirement has forced George to venture outside his castle. That's been part of his painful struggle so far. Now Dave has given George permission to think even further outside his comfort zone and consider something he never could have imagined just a short time before. George immediately responded with an idea that was bigger than himself: using his gifts and experience to impact other people in a new way. This idea excited and scared him at the same time. This vision will empower him to take greater control over his circumstances. It will give him a road map to a fulfilling future.

For most of us, retirement is a significant step outside our comfort zone. Many of our old routines and habits are shattered. New freedoms often leave us disoriented. Our identities, once tied to our careers, are in danger of being erased. This book gives you the tools to move confidently and successfully beyond the walls of your castle as you consider the life changes caused by retirement.

If you have worked through the exercises in each chapter so far, you have done a fair amount of preparation to help yourself recognize your encore. You have raised the gate, lowered the drawbridge, and taken a tentative step toward emerging from your castle and exploring new territory. Well done! But be aware: I often see potential Encore Curve retirees falter right at this point and shrink back behind their castle walls. They can see areas of giftedness and passion, and they know their standards, but they have a hard time seeing how those all fit together. Let me encourage you to keep pressing forward as you take the next step toward building your Encore Curve Road Map.

I know that thinking through some of these exercises is difficult for many people, or at least not natural. That's OK, and that's why we have included sample answers and cheat sheets on our website, EncoreCurve.com/worksheets, to help you think through these important topics and get the most out of your Encore Curve planning experience. Be sure to log on and check them out.

Building a GPS Navigator to
Get You Where You Want to Go

I said there were three steps to this process: review, repackage, and repurpose. So far, you have done a good job of reviewing and repackaging. First you looked at your life and reflected on the lessons and knowledge you've gained from what went right and what went wrong. Then you repackaged some of this knowledge as timeless wisdom and discovered the three coordinates—giftedness, passion, and standards—that make up your GPS. We are now ready to begin the final steps that will allow you to repurpose your wisdom and draft a road map for succeeding in retirement.

If you worked through the exercises in chapter 6, you should have a list of items that comprise your GPS Profile. This list came from understanding the wisdom your life has provided so far. That's a great step forward. To keep wisdom relevant, however, you must now apply it to your present and future circumstances. You must begin to drill into your wisdom and determine what will be fruitful to carry into your future. As British journalist Miles Kington once noted, "Knowledge is knowing that a tomato is a fruit. Wisdom is knowing a tomato is a fruit and not using a tomato in your fruit salad."

We now want to take your GPS Profile and repurpose it to craft your future. The GPS Navigator will be the guide to your Encore Road Map. So let's take that basic set of GPS Profile items from the five list exercises in chapter 6 and do some more work. For each of the three coordinates (G, P, and S), you should have three or four items that stand out as essential to who you are and who you want to be. Let's get clear on your GPS Profile by zooming in on these items you find most exciting to consider for your future. On the GPS Profile: Crucial Coordinates worksheet at the end of this chapter, rewrite these top-ranked items in the appropriate boxes.

Here's what George's Crucial Coordinates list looks like:

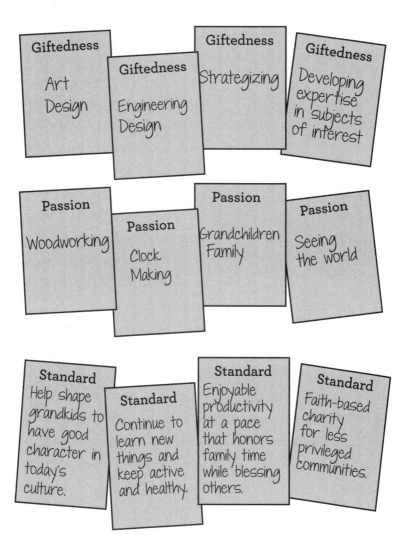

On the page, this list is just that: a list. Each compartment is isolated from the others. To craft a useful GPS tool, we need to discover where the three coordinates intersect in the center of our original circle diagram. In a moment, we will do this by considering creative combinations of three Crucial Coordinates items—one each from G, P, and S. You will start by picking a favorite item—let's say it's a passion item (P). Then try imagining that P item with different G and S items until an idea hits you for how they could combine into something that's exciting and fulfilling to you.

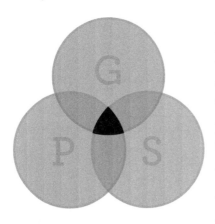

As George was mulling over what his future might look like, he did a form of this exercise. As you can see in his list above, George is gifted at art and has a passion for certain forms of it, but this combination didn't fit with any of his core standards in a way that truly put a spring in his step. He didn't really find his way forward until he started with one of his Standards items and considered how it could connect with something under Giftedness. He values the idea of providing basic necessities to struggling nations and cultures; his talents in engineering design give him the giftedness tools to help provide water and solar electricity. Therefore, a great "GS" connection for him would be to apply his skills and specific design solutions to world problems. This pursuit would even allow him to explore his passion to see the world. When this creative combination came together for George, it gave new excitement and significance to each of the three individual coordinate items—significance they wouldn't have acquired had he tried to pursue each in isolation.

For the GPS Navigator Exercise, we're going to use the items in your GPS Profile: Crucial Coordinates worksheet. If you think better when you can visualize how items fit together, or if manipulating objects helps you process, you may want to grab some index cards, sticky notes, or slips of paper. If you wish, you can print the worksheet from EncoreCurve.com/worksheets and cut out the squares. Transfer the items from your list onto your cards or sticky notes, being certain also to label each item with a G, P, or S.

Pick your favorite item, and get creative with combinations. You can even set a timer and give yourself ten minutes to brainstorm all the serious, silly, and bigger-than-you-ever-imagined possibilities for how your lists could connect. Wander outside your castle walls.

If you found some possible combinations, write them down in the GPS Navigator worksheet at the end of the chapter, then let it sit for a few hours or a day before you come back to it. Meditate on it. Pray over it. Do the ideas excite you? (Notice that I didn't ask yet whether they were doable.) If they don't excite you, why not? Try again, thinking bigger or smaller, more or less focused—whatever seems to move you toward being more excited about your future than your past.

You may struggle through this exercise. Some of us find this discovery easy once we know what to do. Linda already had a good grasp of who she is and what makes her feel significant. George did not. Remember that George had to think about it over a period of weeks, and even then, it took the wise prodding and hints of a trusted friend for him to make the "aha!" leap. Give yourself permission to ruminate; inquire of others; bounce ideas off a trusted friend. There are no right or wrong answers, only *your* answers. You will know when you find them because your future will look as fulfilling as your past.

If you are struggling with this process, remember that you are almost into the end zone. This is the hardest part. The defense has lined up in front of you as a solid wall. But you have come down the field nearly one hundred yards, and you still have the ball in your hands. Look up and see how close you are! Two more feet, and you will hear the cheers of victory.

Please also make use of the guidance tools and examples at EncoreCurve.com. You will also find an online community there that can help you discover new ideas. You will see many avenues to enlisting expert help in finding the right road to your unique Encore Curve future.

Pinpointing Your Destination

When you have narrowed your options down to two or three major, cohesive combinations, make sure you write them down on the GPS Navigator worksheet. I call this form the GPS Navigator because it takes all your possible directions and consolidates them into a specific set of navigational choices for repurposing wisdom. The choices you write in your GPS Navigator are the keys to creating a satisfying Encore Road Map.

Dreaming Big: Build Your Encore Road Map

Earlier, Pastor Dave mentioned a book called *Good to Great in God's Eyes* by Chip Ingram. Chip writes about the importance of having big dreams that empower your future. I think the following quote from his book sums up this idea:

> There is tremendous power in a dream. When you believe a picture of the future, and that picture bleeds out of your heart—not because you have to or ought to accomplish it, but because you intensely want to—it blows wind in your sails and directs the course of your life. It can also direct the course of history.[13]

As I've said, making your future bigger than your past does not depend on age or expected longevity; your future can be measured in terms other than time. It can be measured in terms of the pure wisdom you possess, which you now have packaged and can share with others. It can also be measured in terms of the people you can impact. You can begin to see your future as a chance to operate based on your giftedness rather than your weaknesses. Your future can be denser, more meaningful, and richer in terms of relationships, goals, and impact. This is the future you can begin to create as we go through this next exercise.

This final exercise is a little complicated, but it is the key to clarifying your encore and building an action plan to transform your biggest dreams and plans into reality. At the end of this chapter is a two-step worksheet divided into two time periods. For this exercise, I want you to think of your future in terms of these two distinct periods. The first period (Step 1) is the one furthest in the future. It starts three years from today and extends three more years into your future to a point six years from now. This period will be the time when you are actively accomplishing your greatest Encore Curve goals. The second period (Step 2) starts now and ends three years from today. This phase is your time of preparation.

First, let me give you a little background. I learned this type of exercise from Dan Sullivan, who was my business coach for several years in his Strategic Coach® program. He has been the inspiration for much of my thinking in this book. I still use this exercise personally, and I normally update it several times per year. When I first did this exercise, I was sixty years old. The period covering the shorter term was everything in the next ten years, from ages sixty to seventy. The longer-term period started when I was seventy, ten years into the future, and ended when I was eighty. At the time, I was planning for my biggest accomplishments and biggest impact to happen between ages seventy and eighty, while the ten years between ages sixty and seventy were the time to prepare to make that impact.

Think back to the beginning of this book and the illustration about attending a concert, with the band coming back on stage for an encore and performing their most memorable song. Now think about the later period on your worksheet (Step 1) as the time of your encore performance. The nearer time period (Step 2) is the rehearsal or preparation time. To master a great performance, you have to practice and get everything right before going on stage.

The importance of this exercise is that it implies that you can still accomplish great things in your life. It allows you to define your big, long-term dreams. It also gives you a basis for building an action plan to make those dreams come true *and* demonstrates that you have time to prepare for the accomplishment. For instance, George is beginning to dream big dreams, so now his goal list includes both creating artistic clocks and contributing design-engineering skills to sustainable infrastructure in the developing world. Yet he realizes his woodworking skills are only self-taught, and he has no current knowledge or connections with organizations already aiding impoverished nations. This exercise encourages him to take the actions necessary to polish his woodworking and artistic skills, as well as to make the switch from a corporate world to a nonprofit mission organization. He may need to take a woodworking class or join a co-op community of artists to push his talents and skills further. He will also need to cultivate knowledge and connections with nonprofits already in the field and study the specific requirements and obstacles for each project. He may even need to learn how to raise money and find backers to make his dreams come to light if such avenues aren't already in place.

Several years ago, I decided to run a half marathon with my two daughters and their husbands. Since I had never run more than three miles, I couldn't just go out and run thirteen. I had to train. So I began attending a weekly coaching program. I lost weight. I worked out. I took the next six months to prepare so I could meet my goal of running the race. That's how this next exercise is designed. The near-term time period is the get-ready stage, and the later period is the goal-achievement stage. This kind of thinking gave me a whole new perspective on what I could accomplish in my life. I hope it does the same for you. But don't get ahead of me; let me lead you through it.

> So just dream big. Think for a minute about the biggest, wildest goals and dreams you have ever thought of. Assume there are no barriers to these dreams.

Your Big, Hairy, Audacious Goals

You can find these worksheets at the end of this chapter and full-size versions at EncoreCurve.com/worksheets.

We are going to start with the later time frame—Step 1—of the Encore Road Map Exercise described above. To help you focus on specific actions for your biggest goals, Step 1 lists only a three-year period. But don't allow the three years to limit your dreaming. This period will launch the most important things you want to accomplish during the rest of your life—your encore. These are sometimes referred to as your "big, hairy, audacious goals" (BHAG) or your "bucket list." There is no pressure to perform right away since, according to our exercise, you will not accomplish these goals until at least three years from now. So just dream big. Think for a minute about the biggest, wildest goals and dreams you have ever thought of. Assume there are no barriers to these dreams. Use the ideas you wrote in your GPS Navigator as well as any related ideas or new ones that come to mind. These goals could range from traveling somewhere to starting a mission venture to learning something new to giving away a lot of money. Don't limit yourself. Set a timer for five minutes, and write these dreams down as fast as you can. Don't think too hard or try to edit. Just write down what pops into your mind. Ready? Go.

Did you come back after five minutes? Or did you keep writing? I know you might not be finished, but that's OK. I also know that you may have written down things that surprised you. That's a good thing. Now I want you to look at your list and circle the three most important goals you wrote down. If you could accomplish these three things, how would you feel about your significance? Did you come up with something different or more specific than what you wrote in the GPS Navigator? We often continue to fine-tune or expand our dreams as we review them, and this is a really good reason to review them often!

It's really exciting when you let yourself dream and think big thoughts like this. Now I want to bring you back to reality with Step 2. We need to figure out how we are going to make all these wonderful aspirations come true.

Your Preparation

Step 2 of the Encore Road Map Worksheet is the preparation stage. I want you to now list any actions that need to occur over the next three years to make your first list—your BHAG list—possible.

Let me give you an example of what I mean. Several years ago, I decided that I wanted to write a book. What did I have to do to get prepared? I took some creative writing classes. I began attending writing workshops. I interviewed several writers. I also realized that I needed to train my mind with better habits. So I turned off the television at night and began reading books with content that would help me. It's very exciting to make a list of big goals and dreams. But it often takes good old-fashioned discipline and work to make those dreams a reality.

You're going to put in the time and live the next three years anyway. You might as well spend those years getting ready for the greatest encore you could possibly make.

In this last exercise, I want you to make a list of those things that will prepare you to claim the big dreams you just wrote down. These could be actions, new habits, classes, or anything you can think of that will move you down the road toward achieving your new dreams. They could also include obstacles that may keep you from achieving your BHAG. I know you thought that when you retired, you could begin to relax and do anything you wanted. Well, you just wrote down what you wanted. Now I want to challenge you to go get it.

You've heard the best things in life are free, but I've discovered that the greatest things in life don't come cheap; they require effort. Think of it this way. You're going to put in the time and live the next three years anyway. You might as well spend those years getting ready for the greatest encore you could possibly make. So take five minutes, and tell yourself what you need to do over the next three years to make your dreams come true.

Three things will help you make progress. First, think of the exercise you just completed as the start, not the finish. Continue to work on your Encore Road Map Exercise, and keep adding to and refining both your GPS Navigator and your preparation steps. As I said, I've been reviewing and revising my plan almost quarterly for several years. Designate a time during the month when you habitually look at what you have written down and how you are progressing.

And here's another important thought: dare to get someone else engaged in your goals, especially your spouse if you are married. Sit down with each other, and make a planning list as a couple. You are in this together, so you operate better as a team. Finally, if you haven't already done so, go to EncoreCurve.com. There you will find a whole suite of tools and worksheets to keep you going. If you register and leave your e-mail address, I will routinely send you ideas, encouragements, and some accountability reminders.

So what happens when you've finally begun to understand what your encore looks and sounds like—when you can smell the aroma of it just around the corner, and your mouth starts salivating for a taste? Now you're ready to see how the money part of the puzzle will support your dreams.

That's right where the Morrises are. George and Linda know what they want from their future. Can they afford it? They will need to take several steps to find out.

GPS PROFILE: CRUCIAL COORDINATES WORKSHEET
ZOOMING IN

For each of the three coordinates, you should have three or four items that stand out as essential to who you are and who you want to be. Let's get clear on the GPS Profile by zooming in on these items you find most exciting to consider for your future. Write them down in the space below.

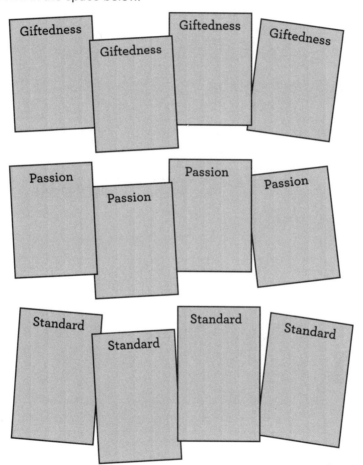

Full-size worksheets are available at EncoreCurve.com/worksheets

GPS NAVIGATOR WORKSHEET
CREATIVE COMBINATIONS

You've spent a significant amount of time thinking about your giftedness, passions, and standards. It's time to put the three things together in a way that excites and energizes you about your future!

Begin with one coordinate and try different combinations with the other two coordinates to see what inspires you.

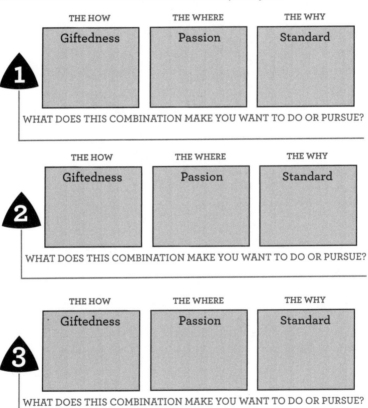

	THE HOW	THE WHERE	THE WHY
1	Giftedness	Passion	Standard

WHAT DOES THIS COMBINATION MAKE YOU WANT TO DO OR PURSUE?

	THE HOW	THE WHERE	THE WHY
2	Giftedness	Passion	Standard

WHAT DOES THIS COMBINATION MAKE YOU WANT TO DO OR PURSUE?

	THE HOW	THE WHERE	THE WHY
3	Giftedness	Passion	Standard

WHAT DOES THIS COMBINATION MAKE YOU WANT TO DO OR PURSUE?

Full-size worksheets are available at EncoreCurve.com/worksheets

ENCORE ROAD MAP WORKSHEET: STEP 1
MAKE YOUR FUTURE BIGGER THAN YOUR PAST

Based on your critical GPS combinations created
earlier, along with your bucket list things, it's time to create your
Encore Road Map! It may include simple desires, heroic
achievements, and everything in between. Step one is to write
down what you want to do in the future—three years from today—
without worrying about knowledge, skills, or financial means.
Step two will address the time between today and your future.

MY ENCORE FUTURE (three years from today)	
Year Range (i.e. 2021–2024)	
Age Range (i.e. 68–71)	
1.	
2.	
3.	
4.	
5.	
6.	
7.	
8.	
9.	
10.	

ENCORE ROAD MAP WORKSHEET: STEP 2
PREPARING FOR YOUR ENCORE FUTURE

In step one you created your Encore Future, which can be exciting and scary all at the same time! You may have some prep work to do before you can achieve the goals on your list. Transfer a few select things from your Encore Future sheet here and then list some steps needed to move you closer to the goal. Examples might include saving money, learning a new skill, attending classes, and researching trends.

STEPS TO PREPARE FOR FUTURE (the next three years)		
Year Range (i.e. 2017–2020)		
Age Range (i.e. 65–68)		
1.	Step:	
	Step:	
	Step:	
	Step:	
2.	Step:	
	Step:	
	Step:	
	Step:	
3.	Step:	
	Step:	
	Step:	
	Step:	
4.	Step:	
	Step:	
	Step:	
	Step:	

A Money Plan That Lets You Sleep

9

Climb the Retirement Mountain

"Retirement is like a long vacation in Las Vegas. The goal is to enjoy it to the fullest, but not so fully that you run out of money."

—*Jonathan Clements, finance writer*

As he drove the SUV to the first meeting with the financial planner Robert had recommended, George considered how far he had come in just a few weeks. The life plan worksheets from Pastor Dave had really helped George and Linda bring their future goals into focus on paper. George was looking forward to pursuing art again, and the more he looked into the possibility of sharing his engineering know-how with others around the world, the more excited he became about retiring. He had narrowed down his choice of philanthropic organizations to Engineers Without Borders or Samaritan's Purse. He was now ready to tackle the daunting task of getting his and Linda's financial life in order.

Next to him, Linda adjusted the air-conditioning vent away from her. She sorted and tidied the items in the console between the seats. What she didn't do was talk.

"Lin? Are you OK?"

"I know we need help, George, but now that we're going there, I have to tell you—I'm unsettled about handing over the reins of our finances to someone else. We've worked hard on our goals. How do we know if these planners will get us the best rates of return and have our best interests in mind? What if this meeting is just a high-pressure sales job?"

The way Linda had been dragging her feet all morning had puzzled him. Throughout the discovery process, she had remained committed to her plans, and she had grown even clearer about her passion for helping others. Financial matters were nothing new to her. So why were her feet stuck in the mud? George merely turned on the blinker and kept his mouth shut. He had been married to Linda long enough to know that she would fill him in only when she was ready.

Pulling into a parking space, he put the car in park and turned off the engine. "Robert couldn't say enough good about what Mike has done for him," he said. "Let's just hear what he has to say before making a judgment."

After George and Linda walked into the office, a pleasant receptionist led them into a bright conference room and handed them a short document asking for their names, dates of birth, and other basic data. There was also a section asking about their primary goals and financial-planning experience. They took a seat and began filling out the paperwork. Just as George and Linda finished answering the questions, a well-dressed, middle-aged man and a professional-looking younger woman walked in and greeted them warmly.

Mike introduced himself and the woman, whose name was Sarah. "Sarah is also a financial planner here in our practice, and we like to work together as a team, if that's OK with you," he said. "We want to make sure we hear everything, and we've found that two heads and two sets of ears are better than one."

George stood and shook Mike's and Sarah's hands. "Robert Nelson highly recommended you, but this is all new to us," he said. He was glad for Sarah's presence and for the professionalism of the office, thinking those details would put Linda at ease. Next to him, though, Linda put her hands in her lap.

"Do you mind if I ask something first?" Linda asked. "I'm just wondering how all this works. Will we get shuffled around with different people here? What exactly can we expect?"

"Linda, Mike and I have been working together as partners for several years, and we work directly with our clients as a team," Sarah said. "He has been doing this for over twenty years, and he focuses on big-picture strategy and managing investments. I am a CPA as well as a Certified Financial Planner®, so I'm more comfortable working with the details, building the plans, and monitoring your progress. We like to say that Mike is great at flying over the forest and making sure the trees are lined up, while I go down and examine the bark. We have an administrative staff of five people who support us, and we all work together to focus on each client individually."

"I like that approach," George said. He wanted Linda to feel comfortable with the process. He looked her way to encourage her response.

"That seems reasonable," she said.

George hoped that Mike and Sarah, having no knowledge of Linda's usual demeanor, would take no offense from her uncharacteristically small smile.

Mike replied with an easygoing air. "It will be less painful than going to the dentist's office, I promise." He and Sarah sat down opposite them. "I often find that the best way to start is just to talk, get to know each other, and see if we are a good match to work together. As you know, we work with a lot of people who are retired or planning retirement. Basically, we help our clients build financial plans and retirement strategies, and we also help them manage their investments on an ongoing basis. With that in mind, let me ask you a question. How do you think we can best be of value to you?"

"There are just so many details and unknowns for retirement," George said. "We need help sorting it all out."

"But we also don't want to get in over our heads by spending more money to manage our retirement funds than we can afford," Linda said. "We've always managed our finances ourselves."

"I'm glad to hear that," Sarah said. "It sounds like you are appropriately cautious and will likely have good knowledge about your assets and how they work."

"Absolutely," added Mike. "That's what we're here for. We have only about two hundred clients, not thousands. Most of them are retired or near retirement. All of our new clients come to us through referrals and introductions from people like Robert. We become teammates with each client. We bring certain experience and knowledge, and you bring your own unique goals, obstacles, and money. So, for instance, what would you say are your biggest priorities?"

George told Mike and Sarah about the possibility of his forced early retirement and their aspirations for their future. "We want to make sure that we will have enough income without me or Linda having to go back to working, especially at something we don't want to do," he said.

"You obviously have given this a lot of thought," Mike said. "You two are really ahead of a lot of people at this stage in the game."

"We've been doing a lot of introspection and planning over the past few weeks," George said.

"And you'll find that it will really pay off," Mike responded. "Let me show you—"

"Excuse me for interrupting, Mike," Linda said, cutting in. "I wanted to add that we also want my mother to be able to stay in her home and have the care she needs. Although she still has income, it's not enough to cover her current help. It would wipe out her assets if we weren't helping."

The reason for Linda's reticence about coming today flashed in front of George like a neon sign. He chided himself for being so caught up in his own interests and planning that he had missed the importance of it. He turned to Linda and asked, "Is our biggest priority that she stays at home or that she has the care she needs, Lin? I think that's really two questions, don't you?"

Linda's jaw tightened. George wished he had figured this out at home so they could have discussed it in private. Now he had probably embarrassed her on top of misunderstanding her top priority.

"She has always asked to keep her home and to stay in a familiar environment," Linda said. "I thought one of the reasons we're here is to figure out how to afford it for her."

Mike clasped his hands in front of him on the conference table. "Is it safe to assume that her care is also a stretch for your budget at the moment?"

George nodded. "And I'm afraid that means it will stretch our retirement budget even more," he said.

Mike looked from George to Linda and back. George could see that he was thinking over what to say next.

"Linda," Mike said finally, "we have lots to share with you on how this process works, but maybe it will help if first you share your main concerns."

George could tell that Linda was sizing Mike up.

"Honestly," she finally said, "I'm angry that the company has put us in this position with their timing. If we were sticking to our original plan, I could use some of our savings to keep Mom at home like she wishes and not worry about it so much. She may not live more than another year or two, but we just don't know. She could live a lot longer and need even more care. But because the company decided to merge and restructure this year of all years, I feel like they are ripping all our options out of my hands."

"I can understand your frustration," Sarah said.

"And beyond that—and, of course, beyond my need to control certain details—the truth of it is," Linda said, softening a bit as she admitted her weakness, "that I can't stop thinking about my mother's situation. She has far outlived my father, and now it seems possible that she could outlive her assets. How long a person will live is anybody's guess, but the women in my family seem to have a longevity gene. And I've discovered that I really want to pass something down to my children when I go, not be a financial burden."

"That's the main retirement risk, isn't it?" Mike said. "Outliving your money."

She nodded.

"Have you ever climbed a mountain, Linda?" Mike asked.

She smiled—a little closer to the real Linda smile this time. "A mountain? With my shapely physique? Not hardly."

George relaxed. "Oh, don't listen to her," he said. "She has enough energy to climb two mountains every day before breakfast."

"I could use some of that," Mike said, smiling in return. "But here's the thing. In mountain climbing, the priorities and main concerns that you plan for as you ascend differ greatly from those on the descent. In fact, professional climbers say that descending the area just below the summit is often the most hazardous part of the climb. If you don't prepare for this leg, you run the risk of depleting your resources prematurely. The point at which you retire is much like reaching the summit of the mountain. It requires making good decisions in a hazardous environment so you avoid problems later and don't run out of income sources."

George remembered his brother's words of caution about retirement. He looked at his wife and saw the wheels beginning to turn. Mike apparently saw it too, and took it as a sign to continue.

"Linda," he said, "when you look at the retirement mountain, your main focus on the way up is trying to save as much as possible to build your wealth. You tend to focus on growth of assets. On the way down, during retirement years, investment growth is still important, but the emphasis shifts to income and making sure you have a stable stream of it to cover your living expenses. As a friend of mine once said, 'It's not how high you build the pile; it's how deep you don't dig the hole.' Our job is to guide you down the mountain by making sure you have enough provisions and by building a plan to bring you safely down the other side."

Sarah added, "Linda, I know this is the first—and hopefully the only—time you will go through retirement and begin to descend the mountain, as Mike likes to say. The thing is, we have done this hundreds of times with clients. We know the dangers and a lot of the fears that you are feeling. Everyone is different, but the terrain is similar. We have the advantage of not merely having begun the journey but having seen it through with many of our clients."

Sunlight pouring through the window highlighted little motes of dust in the air as Linda processed Mike's and Sarah's words. George hadn't realized how much his mother-in-law's situation had affected his wife's thoughts about money. He believed his children would never feel that caring for their parents would be an undue burden, but he wanted to avoid that eventuality all the same if he could.

"That makes a lot of sense," Linda said finally. "But how do you maintain that income stream? Sometimes—as the market goes down—won't the income from investments go down with it? Sometimes the market can stay down for a long time. How do you avoid 'digging a hole,' as you put it?" Mike started to answer, but Linda wasn't finished. "And I guess, even more to the point," she said, "if someone else's decisions can alter our choices so much, how do we know that the next plan we put into place will stand up against what the world throws at it?"

Sarah replied, "Those are exactly the right questions, Linda. Risk always plays a part. The market and the economy will always fluctuate, and unexpected events will happen—but that's where our job comes in. This is why we've developed what we call the Peace of Mind Investor Process, which breaks everything up into various buckets or segments based on your specific goals. Managing your retirement money is about far more than just getting a good rate of return. It's about organizing your money to best meet your most important financial goals. You can't control the market, but we find that our clients sleep a lot better when they know they have a plan in place that matches their most important financial priorities."

George wasn't sure he followed exactly. "When you say the process breaks up 'everything,' do you mean investments and accounts or . . . I guess I'm not following you."

"We have found that, ideally, your investments and cash flow should be matched to your various goals rather than being managed as one big pool of money," Mike answered. "Where you put your money, what types of investments you put it in, what types of risk you take on, what returns you expect, even your different priorities—all these things vary within each financial 'bucket,' so to speak, depending on your goals and their timing."

"I see what you're saying," Linda said. "We sort of do that now because we think of our retirement money as being different from household money. So you're saying that investing money for different needs, or buckets, should be approached differently."

"That's exactly right," Mike replied as he drew out some charts and papers from a folder in front of him. "For instance, if you knew that your basic monthly expenses were going to be covered by a stable source of income, wouldn't you feel a lot more at ease?"

"Absolutely," Linda replied as she glanced at George. "But we still need to take Mom's situation into account."

"You are absolutely correct," Mike said. "That should be a big part of constructing this plan for you because we want you to feel comfortable with your path down the mountain. The first step is to get really clear on how much money you will need for living expenses, both regular and extra. Then we can deal with some of the other issues. Does that answer your income question?"

"I think so," she said.

George nodded as well. "I'm following you now."

"Great," Mike said. "Now, here's the framework for how we put a plan together."

As Mike talked, he pointed them to a list of three items on one of the papers he had drawn out from his folder. "From an overall financial-planning standpoint, there are three big areas to think about. One is obviously income and investments. The other two are estate planning and risk management. Estate planning has to do with determining who gets what at your death. Risk management helps us identify and control those things that can wipe you out, such as hidden liabilities, health care, and long-term care issues." He circled one of the items with his pen. "Right now, I think we need to focus on the income and investment issues, and we can address the others as we move along."

Mike then turned around another of the papers from his small stack so they could see it. It was a chart that showed some colored squares. "As I said before, we have found that, when creating a retirement spending plan, it's important to divide up money into different buckets to match different needs or goals. To help you do this, we use this chart I call a Goal Grid. It divides your life goals into various quadrants depending on when you need to fund those goals and how critical the goals are." He pointed at the bottom left quadrant with his pen. "In this quadrant that we describe as 'Current & Required,' for instance, you put what you normally call 'necessary living expenses.' In these other quadrants," he said, tapping each one, "you assign goals such as travel and leisure activities, or paying for grandchildren's school, or possibly buying a mountain retreat. You decide where to put each goal according to how soon the bill will come due and how essential these goals are to your main priorities and lifestyle."

As Linda listened, she suddenly perked up and said, "So let me get this straight. As I said, I do understand how we think of our retirement savings as distinct from our household money. But you're saying that, rather than thinking of all our retirement money as one big pot, we should further divide it up into various pieces according to our goals?" Her brow wrinkled. "That sounds really complicated. Doesn't that make it harder and more expensive to manage your money?"

"Actually," Sarah said, "we have found that these buckets simplify planning and help manage risk and expectations. Just as not all goals are the same, the money to fund those goals should not be the same. Let me give you an example. The ability to cover essential expenses is at the core of feeling financially secure in retirement. These expenses include the necessities of life, such as the roof over your head, utility bills, food, and health care. We recommend that you try to cover 100 percent of these basic expenses with guaranteed or stable sources of income, such as Social Security, pensions, and other reliable sources. You want to be in a position both to know the basic amount of money you will spend each month and also to have a high degree of assurance that the income will be there to cover it. Once we protect this necessary monthly income from dependence on the market, with all its fluctuations, you can begin to relax and sleep better at night."

"Well, that makes sense," George said. "My brother really got hurt in the last downturn and had to cut back on a lot of his important retirement goals. But what about the rest of the money? How do you know there will be enough for everything else?"

Mike replied, "Of course, no one can see far enough into the future to predict every outcome, but once you have a solid plan in place to cover essential expenses, we can then focus on creating solutions that will help meet your more discretionary—or lifestyle-related—expenses. This includes helping maintain your mother's lifestyle, Linda. While essential expenses are those that are critical to living—like food, health care, and utilities—lifestyle expenses are what retirement dreams are made of. Travel, vacation homes, visiting the grandkids, dining out, hobbies—all the things that make retirement fun and interesting. We find that, if we can get the first part right, and if you are realistic in setting your goals, the rest begins to fall into place. Then, after we get all these income plans figured out, we can address the health care and estate issues."

George liked what he was hearing. "That's a really comprehensive approach," he said. "I don't think I'd ever thought about defining our finances in that kind of framework." He looked over to Linda for her reaction.

"Really, it's quite simple—almost common sense—when you think about it, isn't it?" she said. "But that's not generally how we have thought this through before. I think it helps build a framework we can use to figure out a solution for Mom's care and our future income." She tipped her head, and George saw the look that usually told him she was about to show him the flaw in his design. "All this sounds expensive," she said. "What kind of fees do you charge for setting it all up and for ongoing help?"

Mike nodded. "Cost is an important question. We normally charge a planning fee at the beginning of a relationship so we can review all your financial information and prepare a written plan for you and put you on track. And we normally charge a smaller ongoing fee each year to help keep you on track." He handed the paperwork George and Linda had filled out over to Sarah, who began scanning through the information and writing down notes. "To settle your mind, let Sarah take a moment to go over your financial situation so we can give you a better idea of what your fee would be. I think you'll be pleasantly surprised. Overall, our objective is to build a long-term relationship with our clients and focus on their needs. So I never want our fees to get in the way of that. Our basic planning fee ranges between $1,000 and $5,000 initially, depending on the complexity of your situation." He looked over to Sarah, who was finishing a few calculations.

"In your case," she said, looking up from her notes, "the fee should run in the middle of that range—let's say $2,500. Each of our clients is unique, so if we get into something more complicated, the amount can go up from there."

Mike resumed the explanation. "For that fee, we will review all of your financial information including your wills, retirement plans, insurance, and investments. We will prepare a written report, specific to your situation, with observations, a summary of your goals, and recommendations for any changes. Basically, we want to build a game plan for how to move forward based on the framework I explained. Does that sound like something we can work together on?"

"I have to admit, you've offered more than I expected," Linda said.

George said, "That's exactly what we were hoping for. We really need to have a written game plan. I feel like we are lost right now. I'm a design engineer, and I know that when I get stuck on a design, I can get unstuck by going back to the original proposal. I can see a written plan serving the same purpose. One other issue, though. Neither one of us is all that comfortable making investment decisions on the amount of money we are talking about. I assume that is something you also handle."

"Absolutely," Sarah replied. "Mike cut his teeth managing investments and loves that part of the business. We manage nearly $200 million for our clients, so it's a very big part of what we do. Also, we find that having regular meetings with you for reviews and updates really helps both you and us stay on top of investment progress and planning issues."

Mike jumped back in. "When we build portfolios for our clients, we take care to meet their specific investment and retirement needs rather than just try to chase the hot market trends. I'm not so much interested in making super-high returns as I am in making sure our clients meet their individual retirement goals, produce adequate income, and protect their hard-earned wealth. Most investment advisors charge between 1 and 2 percent per year of assets managed. We try to stay on the lower end of that scale, depending on the size and complexity of an account. When it makes sense, we often use some products that pay us a commission. If the product pays us directly, then we don't charge you a fee on that investment. Does that seem reasonable?"

George smiled at Linda and then said, "Even though I don't understand a lot of the details yet, I think this sounds exactly like the type of help we need. What do you think, Lin?"

"Count me in," Linda replied. "What do you need from us to get started?"

Sarah handed Linda a folder. "You have some homework to do first. This folder contains a list of the items we will need to start working on your plan. The list includes such things as investment statements, insurance policies, tax returns, and estate-planning documents. Also in this packet are some planning forms that you will need to fill out. There is a budget worksheet based on the Peace of Mind Investor Process that Mike reviewed a few minutes ago that will help you define what your basic and lifestyle expenses are. There are also a couple of other questionnaires that will give us a better idea of your goals and risk tolerance."

"Yes," Mike said. "It's particularly important that you spend time on these last two worksheets. The first one is the Goal Grid." He gave them a copy of the page showing the four-quadrant grid, which they had discussed earlier. "This tool will allow you to prioritize your money needs into four quadrants based on how critical the need is and how soon you need that money," continued Mike. "The money you need to make next month's house payment is more critical and time dependent than the money you need to replace your car or buy a mountain house in five years. Be sure and work through this tool. I think it will really help you set some priorities." He pointed to the worksheet underneath the Goal Grid. "And the second is the Risk Assessment. Also pay extra attention to completing this one—it will be our first step to reducing the risks you will face in retirement. Unfortunately, for us to do our job, we have to ask you to do some homework. The better you do your homework, the better we can do our job."

"And Linda," Sarah said, "based on what you and George have mentioned, there's a good chance that you may want to explore some different options with your mother to extend her health care dollars without overextending your budget. As you work through this Goal Grid tool, be thinking about what aspect of her care is the most important for you both. As much as you want to help, you may be risking your success coming down the mountain more than you think. I'm not saying you need to change your direction. I just think there may be some other options you haven't considered."

Linda nodded, but didn't say much. After signing a retainer check and the appropriate paperwork, George and Linda scheduled their follow-up meeting and the date for when they'd need to return all of their homework.

As they were getting on the elevator to go down to the first level, Linda remarked, "George, they had a lot of great things to say, but I'm not ready to give up on Mom's wishes."

"I don't think Mike and Sarah are either," George said, "but we'll have to decide if it's a priority that trumps our other goals."

"It is," she said.

George chose his words carefully as they stepped into the lobby and headed out to the car. "I imagine something else will probably have to be left on the table, then," he said finally.

"More to the point," Linda said, "Worldwide Engineering better show up with a good offer."

George was thinking that, too. But he also thought, *What if they don't?*

10

Sidestep Useless Risk

*"Risk is what's left over when you think
you've thought of everything."*

—Carl Richards, financial advisor

Linda made an important discovery in the previous chapter: hiring a guide will make her journey on the retirement mountain more successful and more certain. But she's still hanging on to some climbing-the-mountain habits that might make the descent treacherous. She rightly has a desire to help her mother stay in her own home, but if those costs eat too deeply into her and George's budget—or, worse yet, their savings—at this critical part of the climb, outliving their retirement income becomes a real possibility. Like a sinkhole, the hole they dig for that one desire may suck in all their dreams for their own futures, too.

As Mike has begun to explain to her, retirement becomes much more about managing risks and making choices. In the accumulation phase, you may be able to withstand a certain level of risk in your portfolio, because you still have two important benefits: you have a steady source of income, and you have time. You have time to accumulate and time to correct investing mistakes. Before retirement, you can still climb out of the holes; after retirement, not so much.

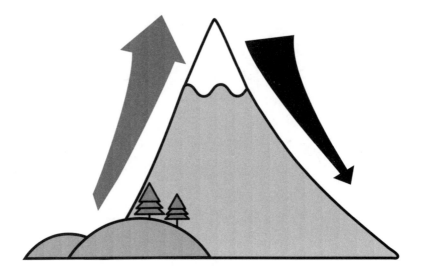

Once you reach the summit of the mountain, you shift from saving for retirement to drawing on those savings for income. At that time, most of us move from an attitude of risk tolerance to one of loss avoidance. We can't afford to dig deep holes. So developing stable income sources and building adequate resources for emergencies become higher priorities than taking risks to beat the market—yet risk is still an unavoidable element of investing.

Let's take a close look at some of the risks that retirees face. To do this, think of risk as coming from two separate sources: the external risks of the market and the internal risks of emotional investing.

External Market Risks

External market risks come about through the process of making investing decisions. They are external because they are related to impersonal economic and market factors.

Useful versus Useless Risk

When it comes to investing, there is no free lunch. A lot of very real risks are unavoidable. You cannot gain investment returns without incurring investment risks. Theoretically, the greater your desired return, the greater the amount of risk you must be willing to accept. But what if you find you can get the same return and take

> When asking whether the risk is worth taking, it might be helpful to divide investment risk into two camps— "useful risk" and "useless risk."

less risk? Why take that additional risk if you won't get any additional potential reward? Think of it like this: If you want a quart of return, would you rather take a gallon of risk, a quart of risk, or a pint of risk? Part of the art and science of investing is matching your level of risk with your needed return and being realistic about the return you need.

When asking whether the risk is worth taking, it might be helpful to divide investment risk into two camps—"useful risk" and "useless risk." Risk is useful when it brings about an expected or desired rate of return—when you stand a good chance of getting paid for taking the risk. For instance, investing in a broad market index such as an S&P 500® Index fund will give you both the risk and the return of the broad market—an easy trade-off. On the other hand, concentrating all your holdings into just a few stocks may increase your risk manifold over the index fund and may not give you any greater potential return. This is useless risk because you take the risk without the off-setting possibility of return. Certain risks are useless when they do not produce a potential return that is high enough for you to take them or when you can gain the same reward by taking less risk. Therefore, each risk source needs to be weighed in terms of being useful or not.

Let's look at some common investment risk factors.

Volatility Risk

Volatility measures the tendency for an investment to fluctuate in value. The more an investment fluctuates in value, the greater its risk. Volatility is one of the most widely used indicators of risk in performance-based investing, and we'll talk more about it as we go along. For now, think of volatility in two ways: fluctuations of the market as a whole (otherwise known as market volatility) and fluctuations in the value of a single investment as compared with the market, regardless of market changes.

Interest Rate Risk

Many investors assume that bonds are safe because they pay a steady stream of interest. But they could pose some risks that will surprise you. Think of a seesaw on a playground. At one end is the interest rate, and at the other end is the price of the bond. As interest rates go up, the price of the bond tends to fall. Conversely, as interest rates fall, the price of the bond tends to rise. This relationship can transform a seemingly safe bond investment into a potentially losing proposition, especially when interest rates are very low and likely to rise.

Inflation Risk

Inflation risk is the risk that your purchasing power will decrease over time. This risk is especially important to retirees as life expectancies continue to increase. Assume you just retired with an income of $100,000 per year. At an inflation rate of only 3 percent, your income would have to rise to $150,000 in twelve years just to maintain your standard of living. This means if you are relying only on fixed-interest-rate investments, you are potentially losing spending power each year. This risk is not often well known or understood by retirees who think they are playing it safe.

Emergencies and Liquidity

A client called to tell me his wife had cancer. The illness had been discovered unexpectedly, and the treatment was going to be expensive and take a long time. He was obviously distraught and worried about money. Almost all of his investments were in IRA accounts. He asked whether we could liquidate one of these accounts and transfer the proceeds to his money-market account to be available to pay the medical expenses and related costs.

After analyzing his various options, we showed him how liquidating the IRA would not only make the entire amount subject to ordinary income taxes but also substantially increase his tax bracket and further penalize him. To address his liquidity needs, we set up a process to gradually fund the medical costs as they were incurred, and together, we substantially reduced his tax bite.

Liquidity Risk

Liquidity risk is the risk of not being able to quickly convert your investments to cash when you need to. Some investments—such as real estate, oil and gas, partnerships, and closely held business interests—do not have a readily accessible market. This means you can't sell these investments quickly or without taking the beating that could come with a forced sale. It does not mean these types of investments should not be owned—just that you should be aware they could have this risk. Remember: as a retiree, you can spend only cash, and being asset rich but cash poor can be very stressful.

Investments that are normally more liquid—such as stocks, bonds, and mutual funds—may also become illiquid because of market risk or tax consequences. To raise cash, you may at times be forced to sell an investment when market prices have declined and the investment's value is less than you wanted. In other situations, you may find yourself forced to liquidate IRA accounts that are subject to ordinary income taxes, or investments that have large capital gains.

Many of the decisions involving liquidity risk are stressful because these situations may happen at times when you are not prepared. But often, a little long-term planning and a realistic appraisal of your liquidity needs will keep you from encountering liquidity risk problems.

Avoid Useless Risk

Volatility Risk. Pay attention to this measurement of value fluctuation in terms of the market as a whole and how a single investment can change in value compared with overall market changes.

Interest Rate Risk. Ladder your bonds, and hold them to maturity. Avoid bond mutual funds that could fluctuate wildly with interest rate changes.

Inflation Risk. Avoid relying solely on fixed-interest-rate investments just to lower your market risk. Your bigger risk could be losing spending power due to inflation.

Liquidity Risk. Assess your needs realistically, and create a long-term liquidity plan. When emergencies arise, staggering liquidation and funding the costs gradually may reduce potential losses.

Event Risk. Building a game plan on solid principles is your best defense against unforeseen catastrophes.

Event Risk

Any number of other external and market-driven risks—such as exchange-rate risk, regulatory risk, and credit risk—may affect your investments. The final one that we need to discuss here, however, is event risk. The 2001 World Trade Center disaster is a perfect example of event risk. We live in a more volatile world where unforeseen catastrophes can have widespread implications. I have heard reports that 9/11 cost our economy more than 1.5 million jobs and over $1 trillion, not to mention the vast erosion of individual investments and personal confidence it caused. The biggest problem for many retirees is combating the emotions that a catastrophic event produces. Building a game plan based on solid principles is the best defense.

The Internal Risk of Emotional Investing

Despite all I've just said about market risk, the most common risk most retirees and investors face is not market risk. It is the risk of involving our emotions. We are our own worst enemies when investing our money. Investing is a highly emotional undertaking, and I've found that when we make emotional decisions about money, they are almost always the wrong decisions.

Let me explain. For nearly two decades, an investment research firm named Dalbar, Inc., has been conducting annual studies to determine how investors' decisions impact their investment performance. Unfortunately, the firm has found consistently that investment decisions have a very big impact. The results of every year's study so far illustrate a big difference in what the stock market, as measured by the S&P 500® Index, gained versus how the average equity-mutual-fund investor fared. For instance, a recent *Quantitative Analysis of Investor Behavior* study showed that the average equity-mutual-fund investor underperformed the S&P 500® Index by 8.19 percent in 2014. The results for the twenty years ending on December 31, 2014, show that the overall market as defined by the S&P 500® Index was up an average of 9.85 percent. The average individual investor during the same period of time gained only 5.19 percent.[14] That's a performance gap of nearly five percentage points. So over the past twenty years,

Isn't it interesting that we eat too much, can't kick bad habits, don't exercise enough, and, in general, can't control ourselves as much as we would like to in life? Why should we expect to behave any differently when we invest?

the market has gained nearly two times more than the average investor. Why the huge difference?

Dalbar found that more than half of the gap in returns could be attributed to performance chasing and other bad investing habits on behalf of individual investors.[15] In other words, average investors harm their portfolio performance through their own actions by making decisions based on emotions.

Isn't it interesting that we eat too much, can't kick bad habits, don't exercise enough, and, in general, can't control ourselves as much as we would like to in life? Why should we expect to behave any differently when we invest? Why are we surprised when we jump into the market just as it hits new highs and the cash is burning a hole in our pocket—or, like George's brother Adam, when we bail out just as the market bottoms out? As investors, we like to think that we act rationally and study all available information before making investment decisions. We are confident we can choose the best investments, determine the highs and lows of the market, and escape the emotional roller coaster that plagues so many other investors. But is that true? Apparently not.

The following chart shows the stages of emotional investing and gives us a clue about why the average investor is constantly shooting him or herself in the foot (or the bank account). Notice that as the market rises, investors tend to become more and more optimistic until finally, at the top of the market, they are euphoric. Then, as the market begins to decline, emotions begin to turn negative until, at the bottom of the market, the investors are in a state of depression. Now, as you look at this chart, ask yourself: When is the best time to buy, and when is the best time to sell? You quickly realize that the average investor does just the opposite of what he or she should do, and it is all based on emotion.

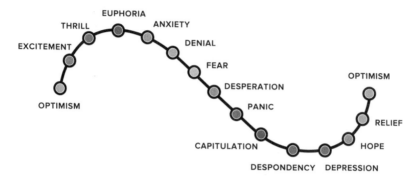

More people have died descending Mount Everest—after they celebrate reaching the peak—than have died on the way up. Retirement is all about planning the descent and not getting stuck celebrating at the top or acting as though we are still climbing. Here are some unconventionally named emotional risks that I have seen retirees struggle with. Look for your own habits in this list, and be careful not to let yourself run out of supplies halfway down the mountain.

The Risk of "Can't Say No"

Many people face tough decisions about providing gifts to family members, continuing a lavish lifestyle even when income is reduced, or committing to obligations that are financially out of reach. In fact, there is a new designation that may hit home for some of you. We've heard of YUPPIES (young urban professionals) and DINKS (dual income, no kids). Now we have KEEPERS: kids eroding parents' expected retirement savings.

Spending Habits

Anna became my client after selling her late father's business for several million dollars. When we built her financial plan, she insisted on two things: a substantial but realistic monthly income and protection of her principal. After several months, we realized that she was withdrawing almost three times more money each month than she had told us she needed. She insisted this would only be temporary, but after one year, she was beginning to eat away at her substantial principal as her spending far exceeded the amount of income that could be generated by her investments.

In a joint meeting with her other advisors, it became clear that Anna could not say no. She had given credit cards to family members and close friends; she invested in dubious business ventures to help out friends; she always picked up the tab for expensive trips and entertainment. She felt the need to buy her friendships and, as a result, became surrounded by people who were more than willing to take advantage of her misguided generosity.

After five years with very little change in her spending habits, Anna's once-substantial portfolio had been decimated—not by bad investment management but by her extreme spending habits. For her, the risk of "can't say no" overshadowed all the good investment decisions that had been made based on her original goals.

It's important to realize that this category of risk is full of emotion, especially when it involves saying no to someone you love. Balancing our own needs and the needs of others is extremely difficult. Many people get trapped between wanting to help someone else and enabling that person's bad behavior or harming their own financial well-being. Linda's hesitation to look at other options for her mother's care falls into this risk category. Knowing where your retirement-spending-plan boundaries are and staying within them is a vital part of descending the mountain safely.

The Risk of Concentrated Positions

As we will see in chapter 12, diversification is a powerful tool for reducing investment risk. Conversely, concentrated positions greatly increase risk for a portfolio. Concentration risk occurs when a substantial amount of your overall portfolio is invested in a single investment position. This is becoming a more common risk with the rise of corporate stock options, stock purchase plans, and company-funded 401(k) plans (remember Enron?). The best argument for diversifying away from this risk is to remember you have too much to lose by concentrating your wealth in one position. Concentrated positions may be a great way to rapidly grow your investment pile, but it's a really risky way to manage retirement.

I list concentration risk as a personal risk because it carries the same emotional baggage as gambling can. There is a saying in financial circles: "Concentration builds wealth; diversification keeps it." Often, investors who have experienced the first part of the saying never realize when to implement the second part. They believe the bounty of the past will continue well into the future. Remember Mike's advice to Linda and George: coming down the mountain is a lot different from going up it.

If you own concentrated holdings in stock because of stock options or retirement plans, or as the founder of a company, be very careful. Think about what your life would be like if the value of your stock dropped by 50 percent or 80 percent and whether a 50 percent increase in the stock value would change your life significantly. There are a number of sophisticated ways to unwind or protect concentrated positions, such as hedging, collars, and option strategies. The key is to ask yourself: "Am I still investing, or has my investing become gambling?"

Too Much of a Good Thing

Waylon was referred to me several years ago. He wanted to retire from a large, high-tech company. Almost all of his assets were in the company's various retirement plans and invested in the company's stock, which had done extremely well. Waylon, an assembly-line technician, had total stock holdings that exceeded $1 million.

When we built his financial plan, it became clear that he could retire and live out his dreams if he sold his stock at the current market value and build a diversified income-oriented portfolio. Fortunately, he did just that and is now comfortably retired, fishing every day without a care in the world. However, when he told his buddies at work what he was going to do, they told him he was crazy.

He arranged a meeting so I could visit with his coworkers. Each of them had at least as much stock as Waylon; some had much more. Each was in his late fifties or early sixties and wanted to retire. When I suggested that they diversify their holdings, I became the crazy one. They had become enamored with the staggering potential riches they thought they would reap as the stock continued to climb into the stratosphere.

To make a long story short, none of Waylon's friends sold their stock. Over the next three years, the stock dropped from $150 per share to about $20. Some of the fellows are now retired but working part-time jobs. The rest are still working full time, waiting for the stock to come back up so they can retire.

The Risk of Faulty Assumptions

Assuming something false to be true and then basing your financial future on that faulty premise is perhaps the most common risk I encounter as a financial advisor. Faulty assumptions may come from our own misunderstandings. A good example would be the assumption that you can pull out 10 percent of your portfolio to live on each year and not go broke.

Several months ago, I watched two politicians debate each other. Rather than sticking to the issue at hand, they took turns blasting each other and evading the heart of the subject. I was about to turn off the show when one accused the other of spouting "false facts." That's the essence of faulty assumptions: they are false facts that we believe are true facts. They do not result from someone trying to lie or conceal the truth. They are lies we tell ourselves by simply misunderstanding the world around us.

False Facts

After a bad time in the stock market, a number of clients called to check in. Martha called to tell me she never wanted to own stocks again because they always went down. Jonathan believed that when he retired, he would be able to withdraw 10 percent per year from his portfolio as income for the rest of his life. William had had a bad experience with an insurance salesman and now stated that he "didn't believe in life insurance." Harriet refused to sell any of the stocks her late husband had bought because, she said, "He was very smart and would buy only the best investments." Each of these people fell victim to their own faulty assumptions.

We are all guilty of making faulty assumptions, especially in areas of our lives where we do not have special training and expertise. These are the areas in which we need to listen to the Learned Wisdom of others. As Mark Twain once observed, "It's not what you don't know that hurts you; it's what you know that just ain't so."

The Risk of "Too Good to Be True"

The emotions of the moment will sometimes blind you to the obvious. So here are three rules:

1. If it seems too good to be true, it is.
2. If it has to be bought right now, it doesn't.
3. If it can't miss, it will.

"It Can't Miss!"

A good friend of mine attended a seminar that advertised an investing system. At the time, he was out of a job, but he was prepared to plunk down $3,000 to buy this "can't miss" stock-trading system. I asked him two questions: "Do you think they are more interested in selling you a system or in your financial success?" and "If you had a foolproof system like this, could you make more money working your system in secret or selling it to others who would compete with you?" My friend decided not to buy the system.

The Risk of Debt

Finally, there is one final risk that I want to discuss: debt. As they say, the only thing in our credit-driven society that you cannot borrow money for is retirement income. Think of debt—whether from credit cards, a mortgage, or any other source—as a negative asset. Assets produce income. Debt eats income. When you have to make debt payments, your assets have to work harder to produce more income.

Debt not only decreases your ability to produce and use income but also costs you money and freedom. When you have to pay interest to someone else in order to borrow that person's money, it is a direct cost to you. The potential loss of freedom is even greater. When you worked to define your own Encore Curve, you spent valuable time describing how you wanted to live your future. Having to service and pay off debt potentially limits your ability to pursue your dreams by eliminating your financial flexibility.

What Are Your Top Risks?

What are the top risks you'll face in retirement? I suggest you make a realistic list of the things you fear could wipe you out. As we have seen, some risks can be controlled, and some cannot. Be sure to review and consider all the elements we've discussed here, both market and emotional risks. Then, to give yourself a head start in thinking about managing risk, complete the following risk-assessment worksheet.

The first step to managing risk is to clearly identify it, so it is vital that you take the time to write down your potential pitfalls. George and Linda need to do this, too, if they want to meet their goals. So that's where we'll head next.

RISK ASSESSMENT WORKSHEET
RETIREMENT RISK EVALUATION

As you think about your retirement, how would you rate each of the following risks? What else could wipe you out?

	Scared Stiff	Manageable		No Problem	
Longevity I Outlive my money?	1	2	3	4	5
Longevity II Die too soon?	1	2	3	4	5
Inflation Lose spending power?	1	2	3	4	5
Market Volatility Lose money in another crash?	1	2	3	4	5
Withdrawal Rate Income shrinks too much?	1	2	3	4	5
Health Health fails?	1	2	3	4	5
Health Care Medical expenses too high?	1	2	3	4	5
Family Issues Family needs assistance?	1	2	3	4	5
Unexpected Events Flood, car wreck, liability?	1	2	3	4	5
Other _____	1	2	3	4	5

Total the numbers from each answer _____

Online tools for risk management are available at EncoreCurve.com

11

Find Your Balance

"Life isn't about finding yourself.
Life is about creating yourself."

—*George Bernard Shaw, playwright*

Soon after they met with Mike and Sarah, George asked Linda to sit at their kitchen counter with him so they could work on the planning worksheets and questionnaires they had brought home. They reviewed the budget numbers Linda had come up with and the goals they had both written for themselves, and they started filling out the Goal Grid. Many of their decisions about which expenses were necessary and which were discretionary were easy. George had no trouble realizing that, if they were going to put money in a college fund for their grandchildren, the fund would be more profitable if they invested that money now rather than five years down the road. Linda agreed.

George had started a conversation with Engineers Without Borders, and the organization had shown him what kind of impact he could make if he were free to travel and work on some important projects overseas. When it came to balancing travel to those countries with Linda's desires for her mom's care, however, the couple hit an impasse.

"It sure is going to cost a lot for you to travel to some of these places," Linda said. "That on top of the home care may push our budget over the edge. And I won't be able to go with you while Mom needs me."

George's barstool rocked unevenly, and he scooted it to another position on the floor. "I know it's a heavy front-end expense, but if I don't travel now, I might miss out on the project that really fits my passion. You wanted me to find my passion, and I have. I thought that was the point of what we're trying to do here: make our future larger than our past and know the money will be there."

Linda bit her lip. "I did want you to do that. But I also want Mom to stay in her home as long as she wishes." On the Goal Grid worksheet, she wrote "Mom's home care" in the Current & Required column and "travel expenses" in the Current & Desired column. When she looked up again at George, her eyes held a question. "Maybe we can use some of our savings and accomplish both," she said. "Eventually, Mom's house will sell, and we can replace what we've spent with what we inherit from the proceeds."

"In the meantime," he said, "you will be stuck here, unable to travel, and we will lose the return we could have gained on that money in savings."

"Why are we still arguing about this?" she asked. "It will only be for a few years. Let's look at the rest of these worksheets and come back to this decision only if we have to."

"Fine." He fiddled with the corner of the Grid Goal. He wasn't sure when Linda's emotions were going to allow her to discuss alternative options for her mom, but he would never get there if he pressed too hard. "What's the next assignment?"

"It's a risk-assessment worksheet," Linda said. "It looks like it asks our thoughts on certain investment and market risks. Then another section asks about emotional and lifestyle risks, such as our spending habits and attitudes about money. It says that the first step to managing risks is to clearly identify them. That sounds simple enough, I guess," she said. "So, George, what do you think our biggest risks are?"

George took a deep breath to keep his tone even. He figured their biggest risk was committing an untold amount of money to his mother-in-law's end-of-life care without a backup option, but the last thing he wanted was another argument.

"Let's play devil's advocate," he said. "Whenever I complete a new design, I immediately put it through a stress test and look for the things that could ruin the plan. So, with that in mind, what could keep our new game plan from coming true? What are the biggest dangers we face that could derail us?"

"Low interest rates and another stock market crash," Linda said. "That's the part that makes me want to shudder."

"I hear you there." He wrote "fluctuating rate of return" on the worksheet. "But didn't Mike say he had a way to keep income for our basic expenses stable despite market fluctuation?"

"He did. I'm not sure I understand it fully yet, but he did say that."

"OK. So maybe we need to look at what else will keep us from accomplishing our goals."

"My head is spinning from all these numbers. With all this homework we've been doing, it's almost like we're back in our college study group," Linda said.

"That was a study group?" he said. "I thought that was a group to meet cute girls."

"It was, and you did, and now you're studying with her."

George smiled. "I could have done worse."

"What a compliment," Linda said, but she smiled, too. "I'll tell you, what has hit me hard lately is my own health. Mom's deterioration has made me realize that I have been letting myself go. I thought I'd start exercising once I quit work, but it never seems to happen. Here I've gained twenty pounds in only two years, and I'm beginning to feel like a blob."

"I've been feeling a bit sluggish myself," George said. "The other day I decided to take the stairs up three floors at work, and I regretted it almost immediately. I can't even claim that it was my knee acting up."

"I plan to live to ninety, like so many of the women in my family, and I don't want to risk spending many of those years in poor health—especially when it's preventable. I have to stay strong to accomplish all of my encore goals!"

George agreed. His stool rocked again as he shifted his weight. "I do so much work at a desk that I haven't really considered what kind of fitness it will take to go out in the field in some of these disadvantaged areas. But I really want to participate with the on-site work if possible. Maybe we can join a club or a class together and help each other solve that problem?"

"That sounds fun," Linda said. "Better than going it alone."

"I think another risk we have, if we'll admit it," he said, "is the way we often spend outside of our budget or spending plan. In our discretionary budget, we don't always include whole categories of items we really want or money we know we're going to spend, and then we spend it anyway. Maybe there's a way to reprioritize our spending habits."

"Like how?"

"Like how you constantly give gifts, and support missions, and donate supplies to the shelters and clinic—"

"George Morris, I have no intention of stopping that."

"No, I'm not asking you to. It's part of who you are—a part I like, by the way—but we rarely account for that large a chunk in our budget. And you tend to want to fill every need for the people you love. I know it's important, so maybe we should prioritize it. Maybe we can pull our spending back in some other discretionary areas and set aside a larger monthly gifting allowance for you to work within. That way, we'll be looking at a more realistic budget."

"More to give? I like that. I could do that. But what about you, with all your digital gadgets and software? You spend outside the budget on that stuff, too—almost as much as I do on gifts."

"True." He rubbed his chin. "But it's not all about playing with them. As technology continuously evolves, you have to spend money to keep up. I think a risk that might keep me from obtaining my goals after I retire is losing touch with design advances in engineering and the tools and software that are current."

"I guess you do need to have some of that at home, now more than ever." She groaned. "So we need to budget for regular technology updates, too, right? So much for cutting costs."

George absently tapped his finger on the countertop. If only he could figure out a way to protect what they had envisioned for their future without cutting out home care for Linda's mom or being forced to take too large a risk for the high return they would need to cover the cost. "Maybe the company will offer a whole year's severance pay," he said.

"Do you think they might?"

"We can hope." Did he believe that? He didn't know. "It's not unheard of, at least," he told his wife. It would certainly give them more wiggle room to fund some of these current expenses as they started down the mountain. Had they missed anything else? He looked back over the list of risks he had been writing, rocking back and forth on the uneven legs of his barstool as he thought. "Let's see. Health . . . spending habits . . . I think inflation, including hikes in taxes and medical care, is another . . . staying up to date with my field . . ."

"Why do you keep doing that?" Linda asked.

"Doing what?"

"Rocking that stool. You're making me crazy."

He slid off the stool. "It's not sitting on the floor right." He turned the stool over and jiggled the legs. "There you go," he said. "That screw is loose, and we're missing one of those floor protector things on this leg."

Linda got up and opened the cabinet above her desk. She slid out a plastic container and handed him a package of the pads. "Here," she said. "An easy fix."

He peeled the backing off the felt and positioned it on the bare leg. Then he rummaged in the catchall drawer for a screwdriver and lifted the upside-down barstool onto the counter so he could tighten all the fasteners. "You know," he said as he twisted the screwdriver, "this barstool reminds me of our retirement."

"OK, I'll bite," Linda said. "Tell me, how is this barstool like our retirement?"

"No, this isn't a joke. We have to get the right return on our money within the right amount of time and also avoid unnecessary risk. If we fail to get those three elements just right—risk, time, and return—" For each element he named, George touched one of the three legs of the stool, then returned it right side up to the floor and jiggled it to check its stability. "—our retirement won't balance correctly, and we could end up on the floor."

"Why do I sense that we're about to talk about Mom's house again?"

George sighed. "That's not exactly what I was getting at, but you're right. If we don't get that part of the equation balanced, we will definitely end up on the floor."

"I suppose I'll have to think on that," she said.

"I guess we'll need to think on a lot of this stuff pretty regularly," George said, tapping his pen again. "It's hard to know all the risks right now, especially regarding some of my plans I need more knowledge about."

"Now you're just trying to finagle another study date with this cute girl."

"Guilty."

Linda smiled. "I guess I can live with that."

***

At the clinic the next afternoon, Linda and several of the other volunteers were cleaning up the waiting room where they had helped host a special Saturday educational event for expectant mothers. As they picked up extra handouts and nearly empty water bottles, Linda's friend Martha asked, "How are you and George doing with that retirement planning?"

"It's a lot of work, but I feel like we're going to be making better strategic use of our money than we ever have in the past," Linda answered. "George's retirement is beginning to look like a wonderful new start rather than a fearful unknown."

"Good to hear," Martha said. "Don't you know—someone having their act together encourages me that we'll get there one day, too."

Linda stooped to grab a napkin that had drifted under a chair. "I thought you and Chad were fully retiring by next year," she said.

"Yep. But thinking so doesn't make it true, I've discovered. I'm fortunate that my husband enjoys his job so much, because when we started looking into it, we were surprised to discover that we were nowhere close to where we needed to be."

"You two?" Linda said. "I'm shocked."

"As good a business as Chad has built, he's a salesman, not a detail guy. We just never put a plan together or tracked our progress. I guess I didn't realize how much those years of spending our savings to help the kids get ahead would put us behind. We never really caught up from it—what? What's that look on your face?"

Linda waved off her friend's concern.

"No," Martha said, "you don't get off that easily. Spill it."

Linda sighed. "We're having a disagreement over how much we can afford to help my mother stay in her home versus selling her house to help pay for her increasing amount of care."

"And you're the one wanting to spend your savings," Martha guessed.

"We agreed it was a priority until we went to see this financial planner, Mike Hartsfield, and now George is pushing to sell. I feel I promised her—"

A woman named Arlene, their friend who had arranged the morning's event, cut in. "Girls," she said, "I couldn't help but overhear your conversation. I have a few years on you two, and I'm going to dump my wisdom on you."

"What's that?" Linda said. Arlene was in her early seventies, and she never tired of playing the mentor to her fellow volunteers.

"When my Herb and I retired, we had heaps of money from the business we sold. So we started spending it. We gave a bunch to our kids, went on cruises and trips, and had a great time. Herb got bored and took up investing as his new obsession. We had been easily living off of the interest, so we figured we were in great shape. He started playing big-time investor with about half of our portfolio, buying into high-return stocks, and I kept spending. We'd protected the other half in a solid performer and long-term bonds, see?"

"Uh-oh. Doesn't sound like this story ends well," Martha said.

"No, dear, not as well as I'd like. Ever hear anyone say that a rising market floats all boats, but a market crash shows who's swimming naked? Well, guess who got caught naked."

"Herb?"

Arlene chuckled. "Like to have bought him a swimsuit, but I couldn't afford it."

"It couldn't have been too devastating if you can laugh about it, I guess," Linda said.

Arlene's face sobered. "It wasn't just the half he gambled with that was mostly gone. Because we'd consolidated the other half into what we thought couldn't miss, even that half shrunk a little. There's no catching up, see? But we realized that playing and having fun gets boring after a while. When we owned our business, we felt like we were serving our customers and our employees. On our own, we lost track of that and just served ourselves. So now, girls, the cruises are a thing of the past, and I make my own coffee every day instead of buying designer joe. But Herb loves serving on an advisory board for a nonprofit, and rather than spending money I no longer have, I spend my time putting on these events and helping my daughter start up her business." She dropped the remainder of the trash in the can and cinched the liner. "And even more important," she added, "we've balanced out our portfolio so that it should be much harder for a single market event to wipe us out again. When one element goes down, we should almost always have another that goes up."

"Sounds too good to be true. How did you get that to work?" Linda asked.

191

Arlene clucked her tongue. "We actually listened to the advice of our financial planner this time around." She winked at Linda. "Mike Hartsfield's the name."

Martha laughed out loud.

Linda closed her eyes and shook her head. "Thanks for speaking up, Arlene. I guess I deserved that."

12

Embrace Investing's Odd Couple

*"Don't gamble. Take all your money and buy
a good stock, and hold it till it goes up, then
sell it. If it don't go up, don't buy it."*

—*Will Rogers, cowboy and columnist*

As George has realized, investing is like a three-legged stool. The three legs of your investing stool are risk, time, and return. These three elements must work together, or your stool won't stand straight. Maybe, as Martha and Arlene discovered, it won't stand at all. In chapter 10, we talked about one leg of the stool: risk. Now I want to focus on investing in terms of the other two: time and rate of return.

A famous movie and later television series called *The Odd Couple* spotlighted two roommates who were polar opposites. Felix, originally

played by Jack Lemon, was the fastidious and uptight foil to Walter Matthau's messy and unpredictable Oscar. They lived together, but it was a love-hate relationship. What does this have to do with investing? This odd couple is a good way to illustrate the relationship between time and rate of return: time is the precise, measured, and predictable Felix; rate of return is the messy, random, and unpredictable Oscar. These two legs of the investing stool are like mismatched roommates who need each other but are often in conflict.

In this chapter, we will consider how these elements work together and how they relate to risk. In chapter 14, we will conclude by talking about the seat of our stool—that is, how to stay balanced on top of the three legs by organizing your money to generate income.

How Time Impacts Investment Decisions

Let's first consider precise, measured time (Felix) as an investment element. I want you to think about the idea of getting rich quickly. Sounds like a good idea, but is it realistic? Felix would not think so. Arlene's husband, Herb, thought it was before he learned the hard way that he had made a mistake. We all dream of hitting the jackpot, but realistically, when you think of get-rich-quick schemes, you usually think of something dishonest or very risky. Most of us believe there is something inherently suspicious about the rapid growth of money. What happens to risk when we compress our time frame? To find out how time is a factor in managing money, let's answer some important questions:

Time and the growth of money are related by the Law of Compound Interest.

The Rule of 72

A mathematical trick called the Rule of 72 is a handy way of correlating rate of return and time by answering this question: How long does it take money to double in value? The Rule of 72 states that the value of money doubles when the rate of return multiplied by the number of years equals 72. For example, $1,000 will grow to $2,000 in nine years at 8 percent, in eighteen years at 4 percent, or in nearly ten years at 7 percent. Money doubles when return multiplied by years equals 72.

- How are time and money related?
- How are time and risk related?
- How can we use time as an ally rather than an enemy?

Time and Money: The Law of Compounding

Time and the growth of money are related by the Law of Compound Interest. It has been said that compound interest is the eighth wonder of the world. Compound interest is the continued growth of earnings on both your principal and your earnings over time. It links rate of return to time. I believe the marvel of compounding growth is one of the most powerful but least understood financial concepts.

The laws of nature can be enormously valuable or destructive, depending on whether you use them for your benefit or fight against them. Gravity, for example, allows you to walk around without floating off into space, but it can be very unforgiving when you fall out of a tree. The Law of Compounding is no different. Depending on how you use it, it can be your best friend or worst enemy. The longer the amount of time you can invest, the lower the rate of return you will need to earn, and, consequently, the lower the risk you will need to take in order to achieve a certain amount of income-producing wealth. That's why we are all encouraged to start saving early.

Think of our mountain-climbing example again. As we accumulate wealth during the climb up the mountain, the more time we give ourselves, the easier it is to reach our highest financial goals. Accumulating over a long period of time reduces the slope of the mountain and makes the climb less steep and less risky. As many of us have found out, shortening our investment time frame and trying to play catch-up makes climbing the mountain harder, steeper, and riskier. We are always scrambling. The only ways to make up for a shortened time frame of compound growth are either to save more or to take more risk in order to get a higher return. If those options fail or are unobtainable, as they were for Martha and her husband, you will have no choice but to extend your time element by delaying retirement. "Get rich quick" is not a plan that makes sense.

Unfortunately, the reverse is true on the way down the mountain after retirement. Money will grow dramatically as you invest and let the return compound over time, but it can disappear just as quickly. If you are not careful, time can become an insidious enemy that slowly erodes your resources. Remember: in retirement, you are going to spend the rest of your life coming down the mountain. If you expend your resources too early, you could collapse on the mountain later with no help in sight.

Risk over Time

Another aspect of time's relationship with both risk and return is in the measure of volatility—how the value of an investment fluctuates over

Phil and Sue Hires versus Jim and Alice Lowe

Both couples have $1 million in retirement savings, and all are age sixty-five. The Hires need to withdraw 7 percent, or $70,000, per year to maintain their standard of living. The Lowe family needs only 5 percent, or $50,000, per year. For sake of comparison, let's assume they both earn 8 percent per year on their savings and both need to increase their income each year to adjust for 3 percent annual inflation.

Age	Hire's Retirement Account Balance	Lowe's Retirement Account Balance
65	$1,000,000	$1,000,000
70	$1,035,000	$1,097,000
75	$1,017,000	$1,180,000
80	$912,000	$1,235,000
85	$664,000	$1,235,000
90	$192,000	$1,142,000

As you can see from the chart, withdrawing too much money takes the Hires further off course the longer they live. During the first few years, the difference in withdrawal rates is small. But over time, this small change compounds dramatically, until the Hires are broke at age ninety-one while the Lowes' funds continue to grow.

(For illustrative purposes only.)

time. The more dramatically the value tends to rise and fall, the more potential risk the investment is said to have. For example, a money-market account or bank certificate of deposit does not fluctuate in terms of market value. A high-tech stock, on the other hand, might be subject to wild swings in price and thus be very volatile. We've already discussed volatility in terms of risk, but volatility also has some important links with time that should influence your overall investment strategy.

Stocks

Volatility affects risk differently for stocks and bonds. In the case of stocks, think about a minstrel playing an accordion. As he pushes the bellows of the accordion together, they crumple into large folds; when he pulls the bellows apart, they straighten out and become flat. In the same way, when your investment time frame is mashed into a shorter term, stocks tend to behave with more volatility and are therefore riskier. On the other hand, the longer your time frame for holding stocks, the more predictable—straighter, like the stretched-out accordion—their return will become. Stock returns are much more predictable over long periods of time and much less predictable over short periods.

For instance, the major market indexes have rarely lost money over any fifteen-year time frame in history, although they can move up or down by several percent each day. Viewed from a day-to-day perspective, the stock market moves in fits and jerks. It looks like the compressed bellows of the accordion. That's one reason prudent investors should be wary of listening to the noise of market data on a daily basis. Remember our discussion of data versus wisdom in chapter 2? The noise of the ups and downs —the daily data—makes us stressed and can prevent us from seeing the wisdom of holding stocks long term. If you are holding stocks for short-term reasons, then you may be setting yourself up for failure. Owning stocks for anything less than a five-year time frame is not investing; it's gambling.

Bonds

Bonds are the opposite of stocks. In chapter 10's discussion of risk, we compared interest rates and bond prices to the opposing ends of a seesaw on a playground. To carry the playground analogy further, imagine the seesaw is off balance and one end is longer than the other. This is how the maturity of a bond—the length of time it is outstanding—affects the price. The longer the term of the bond, the more dramatic the price change will be when interest rates change. This type of interest-rate risk is a perfect example of potentially useless risk—risk that has no offsetting return. Normally, in times of low interest rates, investors are tempted to buy longer-maturity bonds because their yields are higher—but these are the bonds that will typically lose the most value when rates go higher. By buying shorter-term bonds, you may give up a little interest yield, but you could escape the dramatic price reductions and wind up with more total return.

Before we look at how to build efficiently diversified portfolios, here are some summary thoughts about how time and risk should work together to form a strategy for your retirement investing: Let time and compound growth work for you, not against you, by investing early and staying invested. Be realistic in your goals so you don't run the risk of trying to play catch-up. Remember that the sooner you need the money, the less rate of return you should expect. Don't gamble with money earmarked for income or short-term needs—it never pays to do so. The price you pay for liquidity and safety is low return, but that's OK. Don't fight it.

Rate of Return: The Unpredictable Necessity

As I said at the beginning of this chapter, rate of return is like the messy and unpredictable Oscar when compared with Felix, the precise nature of time. Investment returns can be fickle: soaring one day and crashing the next. Returns are driven by emotional markets, and just when you think you have it all figured out, you may get a big surprise. So let's see if we can make sense of this necessary but unpredictable component.

First, where does rate of return come from? Return is normally thought to be the result of three investment decisions:

1. Asset allocation—how various investments are divided up or diversified

2. Market timing—the art and science of buying low and selling high

3. Investment selection—the ability to choose the best-performing investments

> The division of investments among various investment options is a more important determinant of rate of return than either the timing of purchases/sales or the selection of best-performing investments.

A classic study by Brinson, Hood, and Beebower in 1986 attempted to determine which of these three factors was most responsible for return in a portfolio.[16] This study found that the long-term asset-allocation decision explained more than 90 percent of an average fund's return over time. In other words, the division of investments among various investment options is a more important determinant of rate of return than either the timing of purchases/sales or the selection of best-performing investments. While the results of this study and other similar studies have been debated for many years, diversification is clearly one of the most important investment decisions you can make, especially in retirement.

Please understand what proper diversification does not do. It does not guarantee that you will escape the ups and downs of the market. It also does not guarantee the highest rates of return. On the other hand, proper diversification can produce more predictable returns for given levels of risk over an extended period. Diversification, if done well, should smooth out the ups and downs inherent in the market. It's the key to helping Felix and Oscar get along. It can also make your investing life a lot easier because you no longer need to worry constantly about when or what to buy and sell.

Monet Masterpieces and Diversification

Diversification is the art and science of putting together a combination of investments that are not correlated in their price movements. In other words, we want to build a portfolio in which all the investments don't go up and down in value at the same time or with the same volatility. As you will see, the science is based on Nobel Prize–winning research involving complex math formulas called "correlation coefficients." The art is like examining a great painting.

I love French Impressionist paintings, especially Monet's. I recently went to a special Monet exhibit and noticed something curious. If I stood as close to the painting as the artist must have when he applied the paint, I could not tell what the subject of the picture was. From this close-up perspective, all I could see were globs of color painted in a seemingly random manner. Only when I stood back and looked at the picture from a distance could I see the total subject clearly. That's when all the splotches of color came together as the recognizable work of a master.

That's the art of building a properly diversified investment portfolio. When you examine the individual investments, they may seem random. Some, such as commodities or foreign stocks and bonds, are far riskier than you would normally invest in. Others, like money markets and fixed annuities, may be far more conservative. Yet when all these different pieces are mixed together, like the color splotches in a Monet painting, they form a cohesive whole that makes sense. What would have happened if Monet had refused to use red or green because he didn't like them? Take away critical elements of the whole, and you reduce masterpieces to rummage-sale crafts.

Investment Selection: Winners or Losers?

What about choosing the best-performing investments? The following chart is based on one that shows the highest- and lowest-returning asset classes each year for the past twenty years. If you examine this chart, you realize that it is entirely random—good old Oscar unpredictability. One year, growth stocks might be the clear winners, and bonds could come in last. The next year, other categories take their places. So what should you do with this information? Invest in the previous year's loser and assume it will come back? Or stick with the winners, as most of us do?

A study of the chart by Morningstar, published by Franklin-Templeton in 2014,[17] asked this very question. If you invested $10,000 in some of the investments represented in the chart on the first day of each January for twenty years, how would you have fared?

Contrarian Approach. If you invest $10,000 at the beginning of each year in the worst-performing index of the prior year, in twenty years, you will have accumulated $431,770—an annual return of 6.87 percent.

Bandwagon Approach. If you invest $10,000 at the beginning of each year in the best-performing index of the prior year, in twenty years, you will have accumulated $475,427—an annual return of 7.68 percent.

Asset Class Returns 2004–2013

Best Performing → Worst Performing

	2004	2005	2006	2007	2008	2009	2010	2011	2012	2013
Best Performing	SMALL VALUE STOCKS 22.25%	FOREIGN STOCKS 14.02%	FOREIGN STOCKS 26.86%	FOREIGN STOCKS 11.63%	BONDS 5.24%	SMALL GROWTH STOCKS 34.47%	SMALL GROWTH STOCKS 29.09%	BONDS 7.84%	SMALL VALUE STOCKS 18.05%	SMALL GROWTH STOCKS 43.30%
	FOREIGN STOCKS 20.70%	LARGE VALUE STOCKS 5.82%	SMALL VALUE STOCKS 23.48%	LARGE GROWTH STOCKS 9.13%	SMALL VALUE STOCKS -28.92%	FOREIGN STOCKS 32.46%	SMALL VALUE STOCKS 24.50%	LARGE GROWTH STOCKS 4.65%	FOREIGN STOCKS 17.90%	SMALL VALUE STOCKS 34.52%
	LARGE VALUE STOCKS 15.71%	SMALL VALUE STOCKS 4.71%	LARGE VALUE STOCKS 20.80%	SMALL GROWTH STOCKS 7.05%	LARGE GROWTH STOCKS -34.92%	LARGE GROWTH STOCKS 31.57%	LARGE VALUE STOCKS 15.10%	LARGE VALUE STOCKS -0.48%	LARGE VALUE STOCKS 17.68%	LARGE GROWTH STOCKS 32.75%
	SMALL GROWTH STOCKS 14.31%	SMALL GROWTH STOCKS 4.15%	SMALL GROWTH STOCKS 13.35%	BONDS 6.97%	SMALL GROWTH STOCKS -38.54%	LARGE VALUE STOCKS 21.18%	LARGE GROWTH STOCKS 15.05%	SMALL GROWTH STOCKS -2.91%	LARGE GROWTH STOCKS 14.61%	LARGE VALUE STOCKS 31.99%
	LARGE GROWTH STOCKS 6.13%	LARGE GROWTH STOCKS 4.00%	LARGE GROWTH STOCKS 11.01%	LARGE VALUE STOCKS 1.99%	LARGE VALUE STOCKS -39.22%	SMALL VALUE STOCKS 20.58%	FOREIGN STOCKS 8.21%	SMALL VALUE STOCKS -5.50%	SMALL GROWTH STOCKS 14.59%	FOREIGN STOCKS 23.29%
Worst Performing	BONDS 4.34%	BONDS 2.43%	BONDS 4.33%	SMALL VALUE STOCKS -9.78%	FOREIGN STOCKS -43.06%	BONDS 5.93%	BONDS 6.54%	FOREIGN STOCKS -11.73%	BONDS 4.21%	BONDS -2.02%

Diversified Approach. If you invest $10,000 at the beginning of each year equally across all categories, in twenty years, you will have accumulated $510,662—an annual return of 8.27 percent.

Clearly, history shows that the diversified approach takes the guesswork out of trying to predict the very best investment. So take a lesson from Monet. You may not be fond of a particular asset class, but that doesn't mean it should be left out. Just make sure it adds to the masterpiece.

Timing the Market: Myth or Magic?

What about timing the market? You would think anyone could tell when the best and worst times to get in and out would be. That is only true in hindsight. As I said in the section of chapter 10 on internal risk, investing is an emotional undertaking. Trying to time the market and making buying-and-selling decisions based on where you think the market is headed is the ultimate emotional-investing mistake. I repeatedly say, "Emotional investing decisions are almost always wrong."

Successful market timing requires two sets of correct decisions. You must be in the market at the right time, and you must also be out of the market at the right time. Can we consistently do these things in a way that beats the good old diversified, long-term approach?

Professor and Nobel laureate William Sharpe set out to answer that question by identifying the percentage of time a market timer would need to be correct to break even relative to a benchmark portfolio. He concluded a market timer must be correct 74 percent of the time to outperform a passive portfolio (left alone to grow) at a comparable level of risk.[18] Subsequent studies have concluded that market timers need to be correct between 70–85 percent of the time to outperform a comparable passive portfolio, validating Sharpe's work.

These numbers indicate that you must buy and sell at the best time for four out of every five transactions to achieve the same result as the buy-and-hold strategy. Let's assume the stock market has been steadily moving upward for several years. You might conclude that it is near the peak and it is time to sell to avoid the coming downturn. Even if you are lucky enough to exit at the peak, you still must determine when to get back in. If you miss either move more than one time out of five, your investments will underperform.

The need for near perfection in predicting seasons of upturns and downturns makes market timing almost impossible as a successful core investment philosophy. The minuscule number of days that account for the majority of market returns makes the task consistently beyond human ability.

A number of studies have identified that being out of the market for only a few critical peak days can dramatically reduce your rate of return. Likewise, staying in the market for only a few down days can also impact your return. One of these studies—commissioned by Towneley Capital Management, Inc., and conducted by University of Michigan Professor H. Nejat Seyhun in 2005—concluded that "between 1926 and 2004, more than 99% of the total dollar returns were 'earned' during only 5.1% of the months. *For the 42-year period from 1963 to 2004, a scant 0.85% of the trading days accounted for 96% of the market gains* [my emphasis]."[19] That's only ninety key days of gain in forty-two years (15,340 days). The odds are insurmountable.

The implications of these conclusions are critical for retired investors. Trying to buy low and sell high is hard work with very little long-term success to show for it. Like playing the lottery, this strategy has great emotional appeal because it has that "get rich quick" emotionality to it. But for most retirees, it looks like a fool's game as a core investment philosophy. You will be better off creating your own investment "odd couple" and helping Felix (time) get along successfully with Oscar (rate of return) by diversifying.

A Dallas or a Honolulu Portfolio?

Now that we've discussed why diversification is important, let's talk about the science of efficiently diversifying assets. It is science because it's based on the mathematical formulas created by Harry Markowitz in the 1950s that describe how different investments can be combined to produce the highest potential return for a given level of risk. Markowitz eventually won a Nobel Prize for his work, which we now call Modern Portfolio Theory. Let's look at how the principles of Modern Portfolio Theory can be used to create the type of efficiently diversified portfolios that retirees need.

I have been told that Dallas and Honolulu have a similar average year-round temperature: about seventy degrees Fahrenheit. In Dallas, summer temperatures occasionally reach a stifling 110 degrees, and, in recent winters, the city has suffered the bitter cold of windchill factors near 0 degrees. Honolulu temperatures, on the other hand, range from lows in the sixties to an occasional high in the nineties. So if you have an investment portfolio, would you rather have a Dallas portfolio or a Honolulu portfolio? Assuming you are going to get the same rate of return, why endure the dramatic high and low spikes of Dallas when you can get to the same place with the calmer, more predictable variations of Honolulu?

The following series of graphs shows how to blend the highs and lows of a Dallas portfolio with the more stable returns of the Honolulu portfolio. The idea in this process is to potentially reduce risk and potentially increase rate of return. Remember: earlier, I talked about using a quart of risk to get a gallon of return. Well, this portfolio-construction technique is one way to give yourself that chance. The following graphs are for illustration and educational purposes only. They are not intended to precisely measure the risk and return characteristics of any particular investment. But they should give you a good idea of the science behind Modern Portfolio Theory.

First, as shown in graph 1, any investment may be plotted in terms of risk and return. In the next few examples, we will assume that risk is defined as volatility—like the temperature changes in Dallas.

The vertical line represents annual rate of return of the investment in percentage terms. The horizontal line measures the volatility of the investment, or risk of the investment fluctuating. In graph 1, you can see that a 100 percent stock portfolio has a much higher rate of return but is far riskier than a 100 percent bond portfolio.[20]

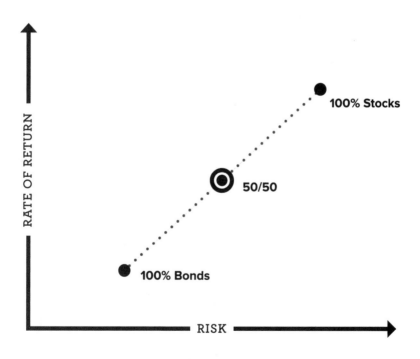

Graph 1: Perceived Risk v. Return

Notice the dotted line between these two points— presumably, it should identify the risk/reward characteristics of any combination of the two investments. For example, if you used a 50/50 combination of stocks and bonds, you would assume that the combination would lie on the dotted line between our two points. This is not the case, however, and that's what makes Modern Portfolio Theory the key to building an efficient asset allocation. So let's look at graph 2 to see why Markowitz won a Nobel Prize.

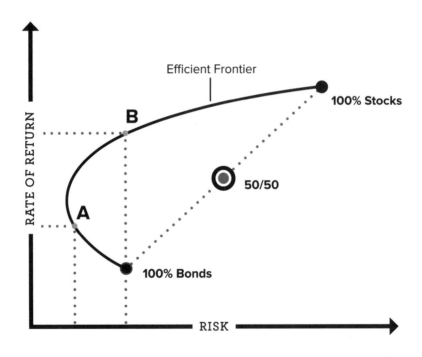

Graph 2: Actual Risk v. Return

In graph 2, I have added a curved line that mathematically defines the risk/reward characteristics of all the possible combinations of the two investments we showed in the chart earlier in this chapter. Notice that as we move from the 100 percent bond point and begin to add stocks, our potential rate of return increases. What happens to risk? It actually goes down—until you reach a point where you have replaced 20 percent of your bonds with stocks, which we'll call point A. In this case, taking 20 percent of what you thought was a conservative bond portfolio and replacing it with stocks actually increases your return and decreases your risk. There is a second critical point on this graph: point B. If you draw a line straight up to point B, you now have a portfolio that has the same risk as your all-bond portfolio, but with much higher potential rate of return. A lot more return for the same risk, or a little added return for a lot lower risk—those are the kind of trade-offs that will let you turn a Dallas portfolio into a Honolulu portfolio.

The Efficient Frontier

To really help you understand how this can work for you, let me dig a little deeper. The curved line on graph 2 is called the Efficient Frontier. It plots the risk/return characteristics of all the possible combinations of the two investments we are currently considering. In this third chart, think of everything to the southeast of the line as the low-rent district; think of everything on the Efficient Frontier itself as the most desirable beachfront property. Notice that there cannot be any points northwest of the Efficient Frontier because that line defines the best combination of the investments we are currently using. If your portfolio does not fall on the line, it is not the most efficient combination of investments. It contains useless risk and doesn't give you the highest possible return for that given level of risk. It is in the low-rent district.

If, on the other hand, your portfolio is on the Efficient Frontier, it is the most efficient combination of the investments you currently are using. Let's take it a step further. If you want the highest return for a given level of risk or the lowest risk for a given rate of return, can you move that Efficient Frontier to the northwest? In other words, can you create a portfolio that is even more efficient than the one you currently have? Absolutely.

In our original example, we used a combination of only two investments: stocks as defined by the S&P 500® Index and bonds as defined by Barclay's US Aggregate Bond Index. What happens if we further diversify these two investments and add some alternatives? For example, let's replace some of our S&P 500® Index with foreign stocks, small company stocks, and commodities and some of our bonds with real-estate investment trusts. Now, you may consider these too risky as stand-alone investments. By reallocating our basic stock and bond portfolio, however, you will notice that we have moved the Efficient Frontier dramatically northwest. In effect, we have added more volatile investments to our mix and produced a whole series of portfolios that are less volatile but offer higher potential returns than our original.

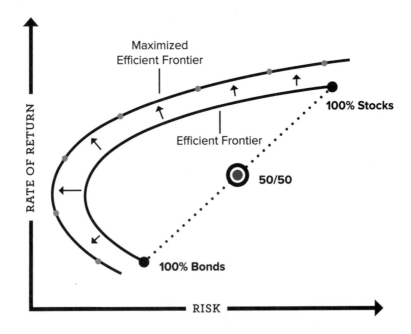

Graph 3: Efficient Frontier with Higher Returns

This is the essence of creating an efficiently diversified portfolio. As with a Monet painting, we have added some additional blobs of color that may not make sense in isolation—but when you step back and examine the picture as a whole, you realize that you have created a masterpiece.

Don't assume that adding and taking away investments always leads to proper diversification just because we reallocated the example portfolio by adding options. The basic principle underlying this example is the fact that every investment moves up and down at different times during market cycles. In mathematical terms, they are all somewhat uncorrelated. The more closely two investments are correlated, the more likely they will move in the same direction at both the same time and the same rate. Diversification comes about by combining investments that move in ways that offset one another, so that when one goes up, the other might go down. If they all go up and down together, you have created a Dallas portfolio, featuring exaggerated swings and therefore useless risk. That's not what serves most retirees well.

It's critical to understand how all this works because it does not resemble what we hear every day. As investors, we may be bombarded with all kinds of data telling us to buy this investment and sell that one. Websites, newsletters, and cable shows promise to make you a successful investor if you will just buy in to what they are selling. Many professional investors refer to these outlets as "financial pornography" because they promise immediate and unrealistic gratification.

Most retirees believe they can somehow execute the right tactics and buy the right investments and that all those random tactics will magically morph into a workable strategy and confident retirement. I believe that you first must build a great overall strategy based on your personal needs and risk. This overall strategy will then produce a framework for executing the right tactics. Remember: strategy should always come before tactics.

Up to this point, George and Linda have mostly managed their own investments, but in trying to get ready for retirement, they have realized that the complex nature of arranging their investments and assets for retirement income requires more skill and experience than they have. They need an overall strategy that matches who they are and what they desire for their later years. In the next few chapters, we will see how they build this strategy and begin to execute the tactics that can make it happen.

13

Confront
Tough Choices

*"Do not let what you cannot do interfere
with what you can do."*

—*John Wooden, college basketball coach*

Tuesday found George at the office finalizing some design plans.
He printed two copies and went down the hall to mail one to
the client. All morning, the office had seemed more subdued than
normal. Doors were closed. Coworkers spoke in low voices in
the hallway. The atmosphere was unnerving. More importantly,
George hadn't seen Robert poke his head out from his office all
morning.

When George got back to his desk, he found a white envelope
with his name printed on it sitting atop his laptop. A Worldwide
Engineering envelope. George took a deep breath. Here was the
reason for the somber tone in the office. At least management had
thought to communicate by letter this time rather than by e-mail.
He wondered if Kim from HR had mentioned to them the way the
previous e-mail had been received and the havoc it had caused for
lots of people.

He sliced open the envelope and unfolded the letter inside. After some explanatory paragraphs, the letter indicated he had an appointment with Kim at two o'clock to go over his retirement offer. *Well,* he thought, *here we go.*

Just before two, he closed up his computer, put his desk in order, and headed for Human Resources. On his way, he passed by Robert's office. This time the door was ajar, and as George approached the doorway, he could see Robert on the phone at his desk. He looked grim. Robert caught George's eye and threw him an empathetic grimace as he listened to whoever was on the other end of the line.

The gesture caused George to pause momentarily at the doorway—though he didn't know what he wanted to say—but Robert avoided any awkwardness by swiveling his chair away from him at the same moment. George kept walking. As he entered the stairwell, though, he heard Robert's tone, if not all his words. He would not have liked to be on the other end of that call.

Kim was waiting for him when he arrived in the HR pod, and he was quickly ushered into her office. A large stack of files sat on her desk.

"You've been having fun all day, I see," he said.

Kim's flicker of a smile had an edge. "We knew it was coming, didn't we?" She indicated the chair pushed up to her desk. "Have a seat, George." He sat. "I hear you got the details of your pension with Mammoth sorted out."

"Yes, we did. Thank you again for that."

"Good, good," she said, scanning his file, which was already open in front of her. "As I'm sure you've read in your letter, your special-projects department is going to be reorganized and merged into Worldwide's own design staff." She looked up and pressed her lips together, speaking her next statement too quietly for any ears in the hallway. "The truth of it is, they were already design heavy and were looking for ways to trim before the merger."

George's mouth was dry. He merely nodded that he understood.

Kim regained her previous objective demeanor. "So, to recognize your service, Worldwide is offering you the opportunity to retire early. They are offering $65,000 as a six-month severance package and would also match anything you contribute from that amount into your 401(k) at your current matching level."

George knew Kim had no control over the number, so he realized there was no point telling her it was lower than he had hoped. Robert had said that Worldwide had spent more on the merger than they wanted. Obviously, the trade-off was showing up here.

"And if I don't wish to retire . . ." George started.

Kim looked at him over her readers. "Yes, that's the second part of what I need to tell you. Unlike some today, you do have the option of staying." She glanced down at the file. "It says that if you choose to stay, there is an opening in production management at the Southside office. It would be at 85 percent of your current salary."

The walls seemed to close in on George. "How long?" he asked.

She looked confused. "How long . . . ? Which?"

He forced himself to focus. "I'm sorry," he said. "I mean, how long do I have to decide?"

"Three weeks. Then they will fill the position."

Three weeks. He thought back to how much time it had taken for him and Linda to make the plans they had made so far, and for the first time, he was truly grateful for the advance warning. He thanked Kim and walked back to his office, where he packed his briefcase. It was a little early, but he was heading home. He had a lot to consider.

***

The house looked different as he drove up. It took him a moment to realize Linda had added some spring color in flowerpots here and there. When he opened the door to the kitchen, the smell of chocolate cake baking cheered him; it was certainly not a feeling he'd expected to arrive at so quickly that afternoon. Home was a good place to be, he realized—and he was fortunate that Linda made the comforts of home seem easy.

As he set down his briefcase, Linda rounded the corner into the kitchen with their granddaughter on her hip, stopping short as she saw him. "I thought I heard the garage door," she said. "Everything OK?"

"The offer came through today," he said. "We have three weeks to decide." He reached out for the baby, and Linda handed her over. "Lucky for me, this little one is here later than usual," he said.

"Susan had a doctor's appointment this afternoon, so I said I'd keep the baby longer. Miranda and I have planted flowers and vacuumed and made homemade cupcakes, haven't we?" she said, tickling the little girl on her nose.

Miranda giggled and tucked her face into George's collar.

Her arms free again while George held the baby, Linda started washing the mixing bowl. "Are you going to keep me in suspense forever?"

"It's not awful, but it's lower than we'd hoped."

"So what are you thinking?"

"My only other option is to commute to the Southside office and manage production at less pay, so I'm thinking I'll be retiring in three weeks."

"Well, OK then," Linda said. She upended the bowl on the drying rack and wiped her hands. "I've been thinking we should take another stab at the Goal Grid that Mike and Sarah gave us. I don't think I've been entirely fair. Now that you're home, are you up for it?"

"We'll need to do it at some point soon, I guess. Might as well."

Linda grabbed their planning notebook from her desk. "Let's go in the living room so Miranda can play."

George followed her into the living room and set Miranda down on a quilt. Linda put some toys within the baby's reach. He braced himself for the discussion that needed to happen—he was going to have to convince Linda to sell her mother's house.

"So I've been doing some thinking," Linda said. "Actually, Arlene down at the clinic did the thinking for me, I think." She sat on the sofa and pulled out the goal worksheet. "You were right to say that caring for Mom and keeping her house were two different things. It's still what I want, but I realize we need to look at different scenarios and see which one avoids digging a hole—or at least digs the shallowest hole. It's just such an emotional decision—I need you to be patient with me."

After his day soured at the office, George hadn't expected an easy road at home. "Did I walk into the wrong house?" he asked, only half kidding. "Where'd you put my wife?"

"Oh, stop it," she scolded. "I still want the house for Mom, but I realize I was making a foolish choice in refusing to consider other options. We've done a lot of planning and dreaming, and we have a lot at stake. I never knew how important it would be to make sure this stage of our life meets our expectations."

"Never knew how big my expectations would grow, either," George said.

"That too," she said, touching his knee. "But I should've. Now that you've voiced them, I see how naturally they flow from your life. So let's get after it." She moved the worksheet so they could both see it better. "OK. So, looking at our Current & Required spending items, the first thing is to move 'Mom's home care' to the Current & Desired column." She erased and rewrote the term.

217

"That would mean we pay for it only if we can use secondary income, right?"

"I think that's right. And that means that our solid, essential spending goes down by $1,000. We don't have to decide this minute whether we have to sell her house. Mike might have come up with another way to fund her care. We'll just have to see—which reminds me, did you include her Social Security and your dad's pension amount in the paperwork of her assets we need to get for Sarah?"

"I pulled that together last night. I'm close to having everything ready for them. Maybe you can help me find the last few bits of information, and I can take it over tomorrow."

"That's one of the reasons I came home early. So is there any goal that we forgot to put in the Deferred & Required column?" George asked.

A look of panic flashed across Linda's eyes. "I think I forgot to set the timer," she said, hopping up and rushing to the kitchen. He heard her open the oven door. "Oh no!" she cried.

"Are they burnt?" George asked, getting up to follow her into the kitchen.

"No," she replied. "Just flat as pancakes." She lifted a cupcake out of the tin by the edge of its paper. It had risen only halfway. "I must have forgotten the baking soda." She started laughing. "I've forgotten how distracted managing a baby can make me."

George took the cupcake from her, tossing it back and forth between his hands to keep from burning them. "Ow!" he said.

"Well, at least they're hot," Linda said, laughing even more.

George broke off a bit of the dense chocolate cake and flipped it into his mouth. "Still tastes good," he said.

Linda looked at him with her hand on her hip and then took two plates out of the cupboard. "These were supposed to be for the bake sale, but it looks like we're celebrating your retirement a little early."

George smiled. "And here I thought I was having a bad day." They took their plates into the living room, thankful that Miranda had not yet acquired much mobility.

"You know," Linda said as she picked up the worksheet again, "I was thinking. We lumped car maintenance into our discretionary spending, but won't we require at least one new car every ten years or so?"

George wiped a crumb from his mouth. "You're right. OK, I'll add the price of a basic car here, and we can keep a little in the discretionary column for adding bells and whistles if we can afford it." He tapped the pencil against the sheet and blew on the last piece of his cupcake to cool it before putting it in his mouth. "You know what, hon," he said after he swallowed, "since you can stand to let go of insisting that your mom stays in her home, I think I can put off some of the travel I want to do for a few years. Maybe that will give us room to expand our options for her."

"But how are you going to move forward on your dream if you don't go to the places where you want to help?" Linda asked.

"I'll have to help from here, I guess," George said. "Plus, I'll have my hands full for a while just learning and figuring out what support systems will help me do what I want to do."

"Why don't we just cut the travel budget in half and defer it a year? You will need planning time, and that will give us time to grow some income. Who knows? Maybe you'll make a little money with your clocks, too."

"A goal to shoot for. I like it. It's a plan." He changed the goal to reflect their decision and handed Linda the paper. "Now, if you don't mind, I believe I could use a little granddaughter time."

Linda smiled. "You're not even retired yet, and I can already see what—or who—we're going to fight over."

George bounced Miranda on his knee. "If we can keep that our only argument, I have a feeling she won't mind."

***

Two days later, Linda walked into the financial planners' office and gave the receptionist a large envelope filled with the remainder of their documents and worksheets. She was waiting for the elevator to return to her floor when Sarah rushed out of the office door toward her and called her name.

"I'm glad I caught you," Sarah said. "Do you have a minute to talk?

"I'm just running errands," Linda said. "Is everything OK? Did I forget to bring something important?"

"Oh, I'm sure if you did, one of the team will call you," Sarah answered. "Everything's fine. This is partly personal and partly business." She tucked a lock of hair behind her ear. "I've been thinking about you and your mother's situation since you were in the office the other day. I hope I'm not being presumptuous, but I wanted to visit with you about it. I could tell you were really upset about it, and I wanted to share a personal story, if you don't mind."

"Well, you're right that I'm kind of at my wits' end deciding what to do. But sure—I don't mind talking about it if you think it would help."

Sarah motioned to a padded bench in the hallway. "Why don't we have a seat?" she said. As Linda sat down next to her, she continued, "My husband's parents are older and have faced a similar situation as your mother. My mother-in-law has Alzheimer's, and we have also discovered that Brad's father has developed Parkinson's. For several years, they were able to hide the Alzheimer's from Brad and me. They covered it up pretty well for a long time and insisted that they were fine in their house and didn't need any outside care. Then they began having trouble. We helped them find some good home-care people to come in part time, but his mother got so worked up and paranoid that she drove them off. Brad's dad did everything he could to keep the two of them going, but when he started falling, we knew we had to step in."

"Wow," Linda said. "Now I see why you said you could understand my situation. What did you do?"

"We began to look for CCRCs—that stands for continuing care retirement communities—that could take them both. After looking at several places, we found just the right one. It wasn't easy, because Brad's father hated giving up what he thought was his independence, and he had a fear of nursing homes and such places. But after a while, he came to realize that he didn't really have any independence as long as he insisted on staying in his house. He was spending all his energy trying to care for his wife while watching her fade away. When he visited some of the modern full-service facilities, he changed his mind."

"How has all that worked out?" Linda asked.

"It's been really good now that he's settled. He discovered that the other retirees and residents are really a great community. He's made some new friends, and he always has activities to do rather than just sitting at home and watching television while he waits for us to ring the doorbell. Brad's mother is fading fast, but she's finally getting expert care around the clock. Because of security issues with the Alzheimer's patients, Brad's parents can't live together in the same wing, but his dad spends several hours with his mom each day. She doesn't recognize him on most days, but he is much more relaxed about that now because they have a support group and counseling for him."

"And your mother-in-law is OK with the arrangement, too? I would think moving her from familiar surroundings would frighten her."

"It definitely took an adjustment period. But I think she is happy with a predictable routine now because she ignores us or shoos us away if we're there and interfere with it. The staff does a really good job of handling her mood swings and affirming her even when she's caught up in some memory of the past. I wanted to tell you this, Linda, because I have been where you are, and I wanted you to know that there is light at the end of your tunnel."

Linda gathered her purse onto her lap and leaned back against the wall. "I appreciate your telling me this. I know I'm being forced to face facts with Mom . . . I guess I had been hoping that we could just keep going the same way we have for the past couple of years. But I know that ignoring this won't solve it." She bit her lip. "Your timing was right on this one. I don't think I would have listened last week."

Sarah stood up. "I'm glad I could help. I'll look forward to seeing both you and your husband at our next appointment."

"Sarah?" Linda asked. "Is that facility nearby?"

"You mean where my in-laws live?" Sarah answered. "Sure, it's about fifteen minutes north of here."

Linda dug in her purse for a small notepad and pen. Standing up, she handed them to Sarah. "Would you mind writing down the name and address? It sounds like I need to start doing a bit of research."

"Of course," Sarah said, then checked her phone for the information. "And if you want, I could meet you there sometime and introduce you to the director."

Linda nodded. "I may take you up on that."

When Linda got off the elevator on the first floor and headed out to the parking lot, she realized that, as much as she had prayed for a solution to her mother's care, she hadn't expected the answer to be a change of heart. Truly considering the options felt much better than she had thought it would. In fact, now that their retirement plans had been forced down a detour—a road she might never have turned onto herself—she was beginning to discover that she actually liked some of the scenery.

She looked at her watch and hurried to her car. She hoped Sarah and Mike could pull all the numbers together, because it was still possible all this dreaming would take her and George to a dead end.

14

Turn Assets into Income

"The question isn't at what age I want to retire; it's at what income."

—*George Foreman, world heavyweight boxing champion*

By now you realize that, for retirees, investing is about more than trying to get the best rate of return. Another way of diversifying your money is to designate separate buckets for meeting separate needs and goals. Mike and Sarah talked about this earlier with the Morrises. As we have seen, managing risk doesn't necessarily negate getting returns on your investments. You just have to be sure to match the risk and return with the goal for the money. Not all goals are the same, therefore not all money should be managed in the same way.

> Not all goals are the same, therefore not all money should be managed in the same way.

For example, think about how you drive. When you leave your house on your street, you don't put the pedal to the metal. You normally drive slowly and watch for pedestrians. Once you're on the freeway, though, you'll get run off the road if you stay at thirty miles per hour. Of course, there are some freeways where the traffic is so heavy that going as fast as thirty would be great. You get the idea: you drive according to your surroundings. Investing is the same way. Not all goals are the same, therefore not all investments should be the same. You want to match your investment objective to your goal. This is part of what George and Linda have been trying to do by working on their Goal Grid homework.

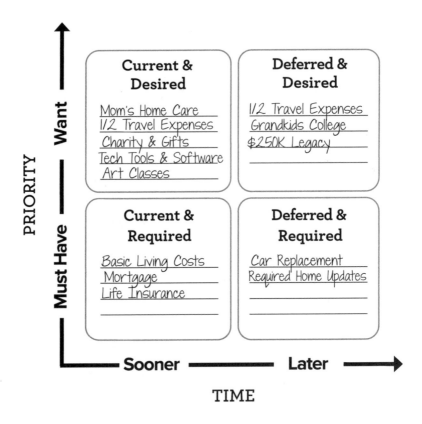

At the end of the chapter, you'll find your own Goal Grid worksheet. It breaks down your financial goals into four quadrants based on time and necessity. In other words, when do you need the money, and how critical is it? In the Morris's example above, we see several goals. Notice that basic spending should probably be in the "Current & Required" quadrant. On the other hand, buying a retirement home in the mountains might be less critical, and the money may not be needed for several years. Not all of our goals have the same importance or are bound by the same time frame. But many of us have never written down how these factors play out in our lives. We will face a lot of problems as retirees if we cannot sort out these priorities.

Wrong Priorities

Several years ago, I counseled a young man in his midforties who stated that his main concern was saving for his children's college education. Then he excitedly told me that he had received a large bonus at work and had taken his whole family on a three-week Italian vacation that cost more than the bonus. When I asked why he hadn't used the money for the college fund, he began hedging. He said the trip was a great educational and bonding experience for the family. He finally admitted that he should have been less hasty in going on the vacation and that, in spite of the great family time they had, it had probably been a financial mistake. Think about what he did. He essentially transposed his money priorities. He replaced his essential and immediate goal of building his kids' college fund with his deferred, nonessential goal of taking a big family trip. He let his emotions override his logic in funding his goals, and he is now faced with an inadequate college fund. His final statement was, "I guess the girls can work part time and go to junior college, but that's not what we wanted."

Funding the wrong goals at the wrong time can be a critical mistake, especially in retirement, when you don't have time to reverse the damage. As you work on your own Goal Grid, think through your many financial goals, and classify them realistically. The example below will give you some idea of how to divide your own goals, but make sure you apply the quadrants to your own situation. Draw on the exercises you've completed throughout this book. These are your plans and your life. No one is going to see your work or place a value judgment on what you write down. Instead, the ultimate test will be how your various goals can be funded in retirement. This will be your first real test for planning how to come down from the top of the mountain.

The rest of this chapter discusses how to balance your investments and assets with these goals. If you haven't already taken a stab at the Goal Grid worksheet, you will find it helpful to do so now.

The Top of the Financial Stool

Once you have a working idea of how and when your goals should be funded, it's time to balance your investments and assets on top of those three elements: risk, return, and time. Linda and George will be working on this process in the next chapter. If any of the three legs of the stool are out of balance or missing, you'll end

up on the barroom floor—a really bad experience, as you might remember from your college days.

The seat of the stool is created by how you organize your investments and turn assets into income. Converting assets into income is the key to building a plan to understand how your income will fund your most important financial goals. A lot of people find this process confusing, but it doesn't have to be. Since you are going to be sitting on this seat for the rest of your life, let's talk about how to get this part right.

Retirement Income

One of the biggest mysteries for many retirees is how to turn investment assets, which we have spent a lifetime accumulating as we climbed the mountain, into spendable income that will sustain us as we journey down the mountain. To better understand this process, let's look at the most common sources of income from two perspectives: (1) variable or fluctuating investment returns and (2) fixed or stable income payments.

Variable Investment Returns

Basically, there are two sources of investment return: income and growth. Both have unique characteristics, and when combined, they produce what is known as "total return." However, retirees must be careful not to confuse the two and assume they can use growth investments to produce income or income investments to produce growth. These investments will do that occasionally, but that should not be seen as their main purpose.

Income Investments. Investment income is the amount someone is willing to pay you in the form of either interest or dividends to own their investment. Income investments include bank and money-market accounts, bonds, loans, fixed annuities, and CDs. In addition, certain stocks paying high dividend rates—such as preferred stocks or real estate investment trusts—may be considered more focused on income than growth.

Dividends and Preferred Stocks

Dividends that are paid by common stocks, on the other hand, are similar to a portion of the company's profit paid back to shareholders rather than reinvested back into the company. Preferred stocks are a hybrid investment, paying dividends that have the characteristic of interest income.

If you are receiving interest income from an investment, you are normally in the position of being a lender rather than an owner. As a lender, you pay the price of lower returns for the advantage of stable income. You are lending your money to the investment issuer, and they are paying interest to you for the right to use your money. They also promise to repay your original principal at some time in the future, normally called the "maturity date."

Generally, the further into the future the maturity date, the longer you are willing to loan the money. The longer the loan is outstanding, the riskier the investment becomes to you, and the more interest you should expect to receive. For instance, a thirty-year US government bond normally pays a higher rate than a one-year government bond. A five-year bank CD will normally pay more interest than a one-year CD. A standard way of measuring how the maturity of a bond affects the relative interest rate is called a "yield curve," as shown in the graph below.

In a normal yield curve, short-term interest rates will be lower than long-term rates, and the slope will gradually increase as the maturity lengthens. Over time, the yield curve will change its slope, getting either steeper or flatter in accordance with the demand and supply of money and with the interest-rate environment. Occasionally, the yield curve may become inverted as short-term rates exceed long-term rates. This situation generally signals a troubled economy and may be a leading indicator of recession.

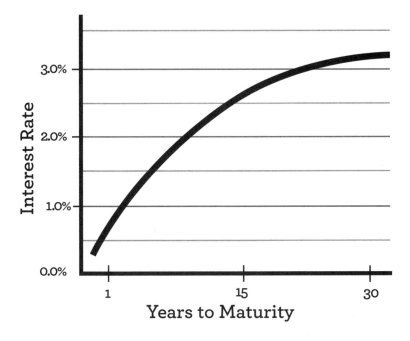

Investment Yield Curve

Another factor influencing the interest rate you should expect to receive is the financial strength of the issuer. US government bonds usually have a lower interest rate than a corporate bond issuer because the government is considered a safer bet to continue interest payments and to return your original investment at maturity.

Diversifying income investments is often overlooked but is just as important as diversifying growth investments such as stock. Because of the ever-changing interest-rate environment, credit risks, and maturity levels, investing in bonds can become quite complex.

Growth Investments. While you may hold some investments for income purposes, you normally own growth investments because

Making an Investment Do a
Job It's Not Designed to Do

When Janet was referred to me, she owned a portfolio of mostly growth stocks that generated very little income. She was taking annual withdrawals from her portfolio equal to around 10 percent of its value by selling stock positions periodically and living off the proceeds. The market had been very good to her, and the portfolio had gained a consistent 15 percent over the previous few years. So, after periodically liquidating some stock and withdrawing money to live on, her net gain was around 5 percent. Notice that I did not call this "income." She was withdrawing principal even though her account was growing.

I explained that she needed to diversify her highly volatile group of stocks and create a separate source of income that was not dependent on selling stock. She refused my advice. She had inherited the stocks from her father. She contended that they were good stocks that had done well, and she saw no need to make changes. Needless to say, she did not become a client. Not long after, the market began a long retreat that turned into a bear market. Not only did her stocks start to drop in price, but she was also forced to sell even more stock at lower and lower prices to maintain her spending needs. The combination of falling prices and forced sales supercharged the free fall of her portfolio value, and she had to drastically change her lifestyle. So the moral of this story is: don't try to make growth-style investments do the job of income investments. It may look good for a while, but for retirees, it is a formula for disaster.

they have the potential to increase in value. Common stocks of large and small companies are the primary component of the growth-asset category. With a growth or equity asset, you are an owner rather than a loaner. As an owner, you pay the price of greater volatility for the advantage of potential long-term capital growth.

Investors often assume they can consistently look to growth-type investments to provide their income needs. This can cause real problems. In my experience, each type of investment should be owned for its own unique purpose. As a general rule, retirees shouldn't expect to get income from growth investments and shouldn't expect income investments to grow. Think of them as having a separate identity in your portfolio. Maybe that could be our first rule for organizing your investments: don't try to make an investment do a job it is not designed to do.

Fixed Income Payments

A second source of retirement income consists of fixed payments such as pensions and annuities. A pension payment is usually a defined amount for a set time period. For example, in my state, the teachers' retirement system guarantees that a retired teacher will, for life, receive an annual amount equal to 2 percent of the average of the teacher's final five years' salary multiplied by the number of years that person taught. So a teacher making $60,000 when she retired after teaching for thirty years would receive an annual pension of 60 percent of $60,000—$36,000—guaranteed for life. This is similar to the pension that George qualified for during his first job at Mammoth.

These types of pension plans are becoming too expensive to maintain because the employer must accept the risk of making the defined benefit payment guarantee regardless of how the funding takes place. Pension plans with a defined benefit are being replaced with defined contribution plans such as 401(k) and 403(b) plans. With a 401(k) type of plan, the employer might make a matching contribution but does not guarantee the resulting benefit. The employee is responsible for investing, taking risks, and designing his or her own income based on whatever accumulates in the plan. As employees have taken on more of the risk of managing the results of these plans, the need for proper planning has grown.

Another source of guaranteed income is annuities. Annuities are investment products built and sold by life-insurance companies, and they have some big potential benefits as well as some controversial negatives. The drawbacks are that annuities can be complicated and expensive. Since they are essentially insurance contracts, investors need to understand how each particular contract works and make sure it fits their needs. Annuities can be expensive because they often have higher fees than other investment alternatives and can have long surrender-penalty periods. As with most other things in life, though, avoid an all-or-none approach based on negative press or compelling marketing. Annuities can be a valuable part of a retirement portfolio if used the right way.

Let's take a closer look at how you might use them. Think of an annuity as having two separate parts. The first part consists of accumulation and growth, during which you simply invest money for future use. That money can be invested as a fixed-interest-rate contract or at a variable rate, based on a basket of stock- and bond-based investments. The second part of an annuity is the annuitization, or income-payout feature. Here, the annuity can be used in a similar manner as the defined benefit pension plan we just discussed: you can turn it into a guaranteed stream of income payments that normally includes the principal of your investment plus an interest rate factor.

Annuities Have Options

Many people think that annuitizing is for lifetime income only and that if you die early, the insurance company will keep all the rest of your money. That's certainly an option, but as with pension plans, there are many other options besides lifetime-only income. For instance, you could determine that you want the income to last for a certain period of time—say, ten years. Or you could choose to receive lifetime income with a ten-year certain guarantee or a refund of the unused balance if you should die prematurely. As with a pension, you can also elect to receive joint income for your and your spouse's life. The options here are almost unlimited.

Another way to use annuities is a bit of a hybrid that has developed in the past few years. Many annuity contracts now offer a type of guaranteed-withdrawal or guaranteed-income benefit. Such benefits are usually added to base contracts and allow for guaranteed growth and guaranteed income under certain circumstances. Let's say that you invest $100,000 in one of these contracts and that the value increases to $150,000 over the years. Then the market crashes right about the time you want to take income, and the value falls to $75,000. With a guaranteed income–type feature, your high point of $150,000 would be guaranteed and might continue to grow at a 5 percent rate. This would not be a cash-out value, but it would define the basis of future retirement-income withdrawals. For instance, in this case, you might be able to receive 5 percent of the $150,000 for life rather than an income based on the contract's lower market value of $75,000. There is normally an extra fee for this guarantee. You can think of it as insurance on the portfolio, much like fire insurance to replace your house in the event it burns down.

These are only illustrations of how these benefits work. Obviously, annuities can be very complicated, but they can have a valuable place in a well-designed retirement-income portfolio. Just be sure you understand these contracts and how they will be used. Remember my point about the Monet paintings from chapter 12. Don't throw out the masterpiece just because you don't like the color red. Annuities may enhance your income if used properly, and they can be a very effective component of an income-producing portfolio. Just be aware that they can be complicated, more costly, and controversial.

Social Security

Let's move on to another equally complicated topic: Social Security. Like annuities, Social Security offers more options than you can shake a stick at. Basically, Social Security is a government program that operates in a similar manner to the defined benefit pension plan we discussed earlier. That is, it promises to pay a certain lifetime income based on your earnings history and the age you begin receiving the income.

Here are the basics. You can begin to take Social Security as early as age sixty-two, or you can wait until your full retirement age, which is sixty-six or sixty-seven depending on when you were born. You can also delay taking the income until as late as age seventy. You can receive your own benefit individually, or you can receive half of your spouse's benefit, even if you don't qualify on your own. In addition, there is a death benefit: when the spouse receiving the higher benefit dies, the lower-paid spouse begins receiving the larger amount of the deceased spouse instead.

At What Age Should I Start Taking Social Security?

If you claim Social Security at age sixty-two, you'll get just 75 percent of the monthly benefit you would have received had you waited until full retirement age. If you wait until age seventy, you'll get 132 percent of what would have been your benefit at full retirement age. For example, if your full-retirement-age benefit were $1,000 a month, you'd get just $750 a month if you claimed at age sixty-two—or $1,320 if you waited until age seventy.

If you begin taking benefits early, at age sixty-two, you will be penalized two ways. If you earn wages totaling more than $15,000 per year, your benefit will be reduced by two dollars for each dollar you are paid over the $15,000 threshold. Also, if you begin at age sixty-two, your benefits will be reduced by 25 percent of your full-retirement-age benefit. On the other end of the spectrum, if you wait until age seventy to begin taking benefits, your benefit amount will increase by 8 percent per year between your full retirement age and age seventy. So delaying can be a smart move for some, especially if you expect to live longer or are still earning income.

Finally, there are a number of other strategies that you can employ to maximize your benefits. The best thing to do is have a good understanding of what you want to accomplish and then talk to the helpful, knowledgeable experts at the Social Security Administration. You can also go to the Social Security website, SSA. gov, and download a copy of your estimated benefits.

Converting Assets to Income

OK, let's switch topics for a minute and talk about converting assets into income. As I said earlier, many people find this one of the most confusing aspects of retirement planning. There are a couple of things to understand here: (1) how to determine a safe withdrawal rate and (2) how the rules about required minimum distribution apply to IRA and retirement accounts.

Safe Withdrawal Rate

The concept of a safe withdrawal rate is one of the most researched and written about subjects in retirement planning. Basically, a safe withdrawal rate is how much income you can safely withdraw from a pool of money and still maintain the capital over your lifetime. Currently, the popular rule of thumb is 4 percent. That means the experts think you can safely withdraw 4 percent of your asset base each year as spendable income. For example, if you have a total of $1 million, this rule says you should be able to take out $40,000 per year. Obviously, this assumes that you can consistently earn more than 4 percent per year to offset inflation in the future. Remember the Rule of 72 that we discussed earlier. If inflation is 3 percent per year, then that $40,000 income will need to double to $80,000 in twenty years or so just to keep up with inflation. In a minute, I want to show you why looking at your retirement assets as one big pool or bucket that needs to earn a certain rate is not the best way to approach this.

A second point to consider regarding a safe withdrawal rate is that it can change with age. Remember, risk and time are correlated. As shown on the chart below, the 4 percent rate might work fine if you are sixty-five, but it could be a disaster if you retire at fifty-five. Conversely, by the time you reach age eighty and have a shorter life expectancy, a much larger withdrawal percentage might be appropriate. Finally, regarding this chart, please note that calculations concerning withdrawal rate must be more conservative for couples than for individuals by at least 0.5 percent.

Age	Indiv.	Joint	Age	Indiv.	Joint	Age	Indiv.	Joint	Age	Indiv.	Joint
60	4.0%	3.5%	70	5.0%	4.5%	80	6.0%	5.5%	90	7.0%	6.5%
61	4.1%	3.6%	71	5.1%	4.6%	81	6.1%	5.6%	91	7.1%	6.6%
62	4.2%	3.7%	72	5.2%	4.7%	82	6.2%	5.7%	92	7.2%	6.7%
63	4.3%	3.8%	73	5.3%	4.8%	83	6.3%	5.8%	93	7.3%	6.8%
64	4.4%	3.9%	74	5.4%	4.9%	84	6.4%	5.9%	94	7.4%	6.9%
65	4.5%	4.0%	75	5.5%	5.0%	85	6.5%	6.0%	95	7.5%	7.0%
66	4.6%	4.1%	76	5.6%	5.1%	86	6.6%	6.1%	96	7.6%	7.1%
67	4.7%	4.2%	77	5.7%	5.2%	87	6.7%	6.2%	97	7.7%	7.2%
68	4.8%	4.3%	78	5.8%	5.3%	88	6.8%	6.3%	98	7.8%	7.3%
69	4.9%	4.4%	79	5.9%	5.4%	89	6.9%	6.4%	99	7.9%	7.4%

Safe Withdrawal Rate Chart

So for market-based portfolios, most individuals would be prudent not to exceed the withdrawal rate suggested by this chart for their age. If you have guaranteed or stable sources of income beyond what is needed to fund essential expenses, however, those can be used to fund lifestyle expenses. Guaranteed or stable sources of income—such as Social Security, pensions, or annuities—can often change how we look at the withdrawal rate. This has to do with how you organize your income-producing assets, which we will discuss in a minute, and it is at the heart of building a sturdy seat for your retirement stool, supported by the three investing legs.

Required Minimum Distribution

Before we move on to organizing your retirement income, let me quickly review another issue: the government-mandated required minimum distribution from your qualified retirement plans and IRAs. Basically, because the money we accumulate in IRA, 401(k), 403(b), and profit-sharing plans has never been taxed, these plans are subject to special IRS rules that require you to withdraw a certain minimum amount each year.

The rules state that you must start taking withdrawals from these accounts beginning when you turn seventy-and-a-half years old. The amount you must take out each year is calculated by adding up the year-end balances of all the affected accounts and applying a factor based on a government-published table. As shown in the table below, you must start to take income at a rate of at least 3.65 percent per year. The percentage then grows each year over your lifetime. It may sound like a simple calculation, but there are some complicating factors that can really throw you off. Rather than going into all of the details here, I suggest you have your CPA make this calculation each year and review the planning implications with your investment advisor. If you get it wrong, there is a tax penalty of 50 percent of the amount you were short in your calculation. So that's a lot of incentive to get it right. Just for illustration purposes, this table shows the estimated withdrawal percentage needed to satisfy the Required Minimum Distribution amount each year based on the IRS published Uniform Lifetime Table.

Organizing Your Money to Maximize Income

And now we get to the fun part: organizing your money to maximize your income. Remember, the more efficiently you can produce income, the more money you will have, and the longer that money will last. Earlier, I used a three-legged stool to illustrate how retirement investments are managed. The three legs that we have discussed are risk, rate of return, and time. The top of the stool—where you sit—represents how your money is organized to provide income and keep the three legs in balance.

Age	Percent Withdraw	Age	Percent Withdraw	Age	Percent Withdraw
70	3.65%	80	5.35%	90	8.77%
71	3.77%	81	5.59%	91	9.26%
72	3.91%	82	5.85%	92	8.10%
73	4.05%	83	6.13%	93	10.42%
74	4.20%	84	6.45%	94	10.99%
75	4.37%	85	6.76%	95	11.63%
76	4.55%	86	7.09%	96	12.35%
77	4.72%	87	7.46%	97	13.16%
78	4.93%	88	7.87%	98	14.08%
79	5.13%	89	8.33%	99	14.93%

Required Minimum Distribution Example

Why is that important? During our working years, we become used to receiving our income from single or limited sources, such as salary, bonuses, commissions, and so on. Both George and Linda are accustomed to set salaries and regular paychecks. Retirement income, however, is often generated from multiple sources, including Social Security, pensions, IRA plans, and regular investments. This can be a big paradigm shift. A common misconception in retirement is that we should view all our income streams as one lump sum and think of our various pots of money as one large portfolio. A better method is to organize your income sources to closely mirror your various needs.

Here are three principles to remember when organizing your money during retirement:

1. **Diversify.** Think of your money as divided into different buckets intended to meet different goals.
2. **Firewall.** Protect money and income designated for critical goals from market fluctuations.

3. **Match.** Invest different income sources to match different goals.

Diversify

The first rule of organizing retirement money—building the seat of the stool—is to think of your money as being in several different buckets that match different investment goals. Our normal tendency is to envision all of our investments as a single big portfolio that needs to provide income, growth, and other things at the same time. Yet in reality, as you and the Morrises have already discovered, retirees have several different sets of goals. Matching your money to your goals means that you should have a different investment framework for each type of goal, not one big pool of money. This is another way to diversify investments to reduce risk.

Take another look at your Goal Grid, which allows you to view your goals from a strategic perspective. The Goal Grid breaks up your financial goals into four quadrants based on when the money will be needed and the importance of having the money available. For example, the income that you need for monthly living expenses is a different animal from the money you might want to spend on a vacation home in five years. If you can write down your goals for each quadrant, then you can begin to reorganize your money to fit each goal. The closer the goal is to the bottom-left quadrant (Current & Required), the shorter term and less volatile the investment should be. The more deferred a goal is, the easier it is to match with more volatile investments such as stocks.

Firewall

The second principle is what I refer to as "building a firewall" around your critical sources of income to prevent them from being subject to the fluctuations in the market. When I first started using the term "firewall" to describe how to protect income sources and critical needs, I thought of the apartment my wife and I rented when we were first married. Between each apartment unit was a solid concrete wall built to keep each apartment safe from a fire in the adjoining unit. In more recent years, the term has been applied in technology to a special computer program that prevents unauthorized access to certain computer files and databases.

"Firewall" is the perfect word to describe protecting your income from market volatility and risks, as well as how you must build protection around your stable income so that your emotional risks or whims won't have unauthorized access. The more you can meet the critical and essential goals from your Goal Grid using stable income that is not dependent on market fluctuations, the better you will be at practicing the firewall principle.

Match

The third principle is an offshoot from the firewall idea: create a stable income source first and then match your other goals to specific kinds of investing. Let me give you a practical example of how to think about organizing your investments around your Goal Grid priorities.

Your first priority should be to cover your essential expenses with a stable source of income. This is at the core of feeling financially secure in retirement. Essential expenses include the necessities of life, such as the roof over your head, utility bills, food, and health care. I recommend that you try to cover 100 percent of these basic expenses with guaranteed or stable sources of income. You want to be in such a position that, if a specific amount of money will be spent each month, you have a high degree of assurance that the income will be there to cover it.

Essential Expenses. To be able to match critical expenses with predictable income, you need to know what your essential expenses are every month. Most of us carry around a budget in our brains, but we rarely write one down. Money is a lot like a four-year-old child—it has a tendency to wander off and get lost (or spent) if not under careful supervision. Many of us have built up spending habits that we haven't examined for years. Retirement requires that we step back, as George and Linda did, and look at these spending habits to get our money under proper control.

Spending Plan

We raised our eldest daughter as a princess to whom the idea of a budget was a foreign concept. However, she married a committed budgeter, and disagreements ensued, with him telling her certain spending was not in the budget. One night, I suggested he begin using the term "spending plan" instead of budget. Over the next few months, the tension seemed to die down. I'm still not sure whether it was my genius insight or the natural course of the relationship, but it makes a great family story. The word "budget" seems to have a negative, restrictive connotation, whereas a "spending plan" seems much friendlier. Whatever you call it, writing down what you spend is the best way to start the process of matching spending with income. On the EncoreCurve.com website, you will find some worksheets and tools to help with the critical task of creating a spending plan. Before you can match stable sources of income to your essential expenses, you have to know what those expenses are.

Sources of the guaranteed or stable income that could cover your essential expenses include Social Security benefits, pension plan payouts, certain annuity income, and interest from CDs and government bonds. These are not necessarily the highest-returning investments, but in this case, you want to make sure these expenses will be covered regardless of what happens in the economy or the markets. Knowing that your monthly expenses are going to be covered by a predictable income is the critical first step to peace of mind in retirement.

In my experience as a financial advisor, this is the single most important thing you can do to ensure your financial happiness. Retirees who know their basic needs will be covered by money that shows up every month, regardless of market conditions, have a significant advantage in the battle for peace of mind. If you cannot do this, I suggest you consider postponing retirement or continue to work part time.

Lifestyle Expenses. The great part of Encore Curve retirement is that we have expectations beyond our basic daily needs. These plans, however, often create expenses, including travel, hobbies, purchasing a second home, helping pay for grandchildren's education, and so on. In most cases, these can be considered optional expenses. You may have placed them in your Goal Grid as nonessential or discretionary. As such, you should be able to tap into other assets, outside of the guaranteed or stable income sources that you have firewalled or committed to essential expenses.

Lifestyle expenses often come in several forms. Some are regular expenses—such as gifting, entertainment, hobbies, and so forth—that occur on a monthly or routine basis. These can often be worked into a secondary discretionary budget supported by income from other investments. A second category contains large expenditures that happen occasionally, such as annual travel or unplanned emergencies. A third group includes big-ticket items that happen infrequently, such as building a retirement home or buying a new car, for example.

As you can see, these three groups tend to occur in different time frames, which should help you designate certain types of investments to meet these expenses. I have found it works best to arrange the assets that support these lifestyle expenses into three categories: strategic cash, income investments, and growth investments. We've talked about each of these in terms of the three legs of the stool. Now let's look at how they can be used to support the top of the stool as you arrange to meet your goals.

Strategic Cash. Think of strategic cash as your backup plan for times when you need liquidity. I suggest you try to keep assets in cash and liquid investments sufficient to cover one or two years of lifestyle expenses. This can help prevent the need to sell longer-term investments at inopportune times. Examples of these assets include CDs, money-market accounts, and savings accounts.

Income Investments. Meeting at least some lifestyle needs through income-generating investments helps reduce your susceptibility to steep withdrawals from growth investments. Set aside a portion of assets in a diversified portfolio of income-oriented assets to offset some of your lifestyle-related expenses. This can balance the need to rely on more volatile growth investments and can also help reduce the need to liquidate assets when the market is unfavorable.

Growth Investments. As you were climbing the mountain and accumulating assets, you probably relied heavily on growth investments—such as stocks and equity mutual funds—to speed asset growth. Now that you're on the descent side, growth investments play a different but equally important role. Growth is necessary to offset inflation and maintain your asset base. In order to maintain purchasing power and drive long-term growth, allocate a portion of your assets to a diversified portfolio of investments that have the potential to grow over time.

This chapter has covered a lot of material. While we have focused on retirement income and investing, we have neglected several other important issues—things like tax management, arranging investment income to minimize taxes, planning for health care and long-term needs, and estate planning. If this is all somewhat overwhelming, I hope you will seek the advice of a financial planner. They are best geared to help you come down that mountain safely—and they can also help you realize when it would be better to put up the stop sign and delay your retirement.

George and Linda are due for their next appointment with Mike and Sarah. Every situation is different, and yours may fall far from theirs. Still, I hope you'll see how the give-and-take of the two sides of the retirement question—figuring out how to extend both your money and your significance beyond your lifetime—can lead to the best possible outcome for your future. It's your encore, after all. Make the most of it.

GOAL GRID WORKSHEET
PRIORITIZING YOUR MONEY

This worksheet will allow you to work through your
financial goals and prioritize your money needs based
on how critical the need is and how soon you need that money.

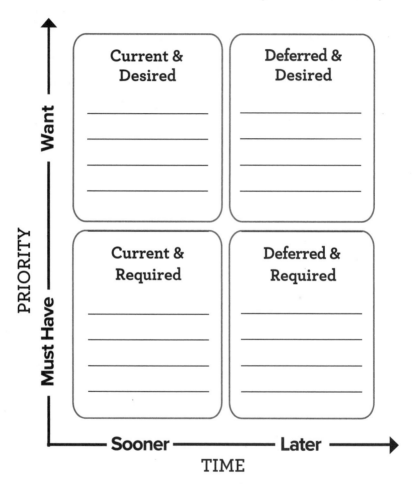

Full-size worksheets are available at EncoreCurve.com/worksheets

15

Match Your Money to Your Dreams

"Now is not the time to think of what you do not have. Think of what you can do with what there is."

—*Ernest Hemingway, American novelist*

So far in George and Linda's journey, I have presented certain principles about finances and life that are both critical and universal as you plan your retirement. Many of these concepts will now come together in this chapter as the Morrises realize the financial implications of their life decisions. The illustrated spending plan used here by George and Linda is intended to be instructional rather than specific. Your situation will be completely different, so please don't allow the actual numbers used in this chapter to distract you. The important thing is to see the general principles in action and apply them to your specific situation.

That Friday, George and Linda arrived at the financial planners' offices with great anticipation. During the previous couple of weeks, they had worked hard to gather the remaining necessary information and deliver it to Mike and Sarah. Sarah had e-mailed with a couple of questions, and George had provided the details of his retirement offer.

"I never realized we had so much stuff related to our finances," Linda observed as they entered the elevator.

"I know," George replied. "It's no wonder we felt overwhelmed. We had accounts and papers everywhere that we either didn't understand or had forgotten about. Just getting all this organized seems worth the planning fee. I can't wait to see what they have come up with."

When they walked into the office, the receptionist let them know that Mike had been held up on a phone call. They took a seat. For the next few minutes, George studied the patterned carpet, letting his eyes follow the intersecting geometric lines from one end of the waiting area to the other. No line traveled straight across the carpet, but, point by point, they all reached their destination. George wondered if he could somehow turn that idea and pattern into a clock. Then he thought about how that pattern simulated their recent retirement journey. Arriving at the final destination had not been a straight-line venture.

Mike hurried in and apologized for the delay. He then led them into the conference room, where Sarah seemed to be making some final calculations. As George pulled Linda's chair out for her, his sideways glance caught Sarah looking up at Mike. She gave a barely noticeable headshake, and Mike frowned briefly in response. George tried not to make any assumptions, but he couldn't help wondering whether their unspoken communication had to do with the phone call or with his and Linda's numbers.

After some brief discussion, Mike began the meeting. "What I thought we would do today is review some of our findings so far and make sure we are on the right track," he said. "We also have some information gaps left to fill. If we can get these covered, I think we can then make some important decisions about a final plan that aligns with your needs and desires."

"We're certainly anxious to see what you have come up with so far, aren't we, George?" Linda said.

He nodded.

Sarah turned on the Smart Board and pulled up the picture of the buckets they had discussed in their first meeting. "If you remember, we call our method the Peace of Mind Investor Process," she explained. "It provides us with an overall framework for creating retirement plans. Since each person has different needs and goals, a cookie-cutter approach can achieve only so much. But we have found that this system works well for lower-income earners as well as for wealthier clients. We always want a central system that we can refer back to in order to be consistent across almost all income levels. So why don't we look at where we are in each of these sections from last time?"

As she talked, she showed a worksheet on the board. "As you re-call, the bottom bucket is the most critical part of the process. Here, we want to make sure that you have your essential, nondiscretionary expenses covered with a stable source of income. According to the budget worksheet you gave us, you need a monthly income of $5,500 per month to match these basic living costs. Does this look right?"

"That looks about right," George said as he looked at Linda. "We were really surprised to learn that our total expenses after re-tirement are going to be about the same as they are now. We realized that, with Linda's mother's care and the potential extra travel, we are not going to reduce our spending much."

"That's not as surprising as you think," Mike replied. "We see that a lot when people retire. Expenses will go down later on, but for the first ten years or so, we often see expenses actually increase."

"That's not very comforting," Linda noted. "One of the wild-cards here is whether we pay off the house. We have a mortgage balance of about $50,000 with almost five years remaining, and the monthly payments are right at $1,500 per month, including escrow. The loan is still at 5.5 percent because we never refinanced it. Should we refinance it, or should we pay it off with the severance George will receive? The company is paying him $65,000, which comes out to about $50,000 after income taxes are taken out."

"I looked at that," Sarah replied. "Most of your payments are going toward principal rather than interest, so refinancing won't give you much help. If you pay it off, your taxes and insurance will still be about $6,000 per year, but your monthly expenses would be cut by $1,000. I like the idea of using the severance payment, but let's come back to that in a minute and see if that's the best asset you could use to pay off the mortgage. Anything else as far as the basic expenses?"

"Well," Linda replied, "we do have a question about life insurance. George and I both have some old universal life policies we have been paying on, and we included those premiums in the basic budget. George's is for $250,000, and mine is $50,000. Together, they cost about $100 per month. Do we even need these?"

"We looked at those and were going to discuss them under the legacy part," Sarah said. "However, it appears they both have sub-stantial cash value, and the interest being earned on them more than offsets the internal cost of the death benefit. One option is to keep the policies for now but stop making monthly payments. They should continue for some time. We can request some alter-native proposals from the insurance company to see how they will perform with no further payments. For now, let's assume that we stop making payments and defer any other decisions until we get the basic plan in place. Between that and paying off the mortgage, I think your monthly outflow for basics will be reduced by $1,100, to a total of $4,400. Does that seem like a comfortable number to shoot for?"

"That sounds about right," George said. "We checked and verified the numbers pretty thoroughly."

"Good. OK, now let's see if we can fill in some of the other blanks," Mike said. "This is a lot like completing a jigsaw puzzle. Let's look at your potential income sources that could be used to offset your spending for basic necessities. Remember, we want to find enough stable or guaranteed income to cover your nondiscretionary expenses. Other than the mortgage, it doesn't appear that you have any other debt. Is that right?"

"That's right," Linda replied. "We were fortunate to be able to get the girls through college without large loans, and other than some periodic credit-card stuff, we are now debt free. We've included in the budget the areas we consistently tend to spend more in, so that should help us stay in the clear."

"That's great," Mike commented. "You two have done a really good job of managing your finances. Let's look at your major assets. You currently have about $200,000 in money markets, CDs, and other accounts. You also have $500,000 in your 401(k), and Linda, you have an IRA account from your old employer of around $100,000.

"Then there's your pension from Mammoth, George. We have a few questions there. I understand that you would receive 2 percent of the average of your final five years' salary, coming out to about $13,000 per year. But there are several things we need to get clear. First, if you begin taking that income now, before age sixty-five, the benefits will probably be reduced. We need to know by how much.

Second, have you asked if there are any cash-out-type provisions that would allow you to withdraw or roll over a certain amount from the pension?"

"No, but I can find out." George hadn't realized that the pension amount would be reduced if he took it early. Somehow, that detail hadn't come up in his conversation with Mammoth—probably because he didn't know to ask about it in the first place. "But if the pension is reduced, are we even close to the amount we need?"

"That's definitely an issue we're going to talk about," Mike said. "And we should also remember that the only pension option we've discussed is for your life only. We need to know what the other payout options are for things like joint life or survivor benefits for Linda. Probably the last thing you want is to take income for your lifetime only and leave nothing for Linda if you should die first. If we can get a printout of your income options from Mammoth, then we will know the cost of these survivor benefit options and can ultimately choose which one is best. Often, in these older plans, it is less expensive for you to cover the survivor benefit by buying life insurance than by taking it through the pension. We might even use your old policies for some of this. We'll just have to see."

Sarah pulled out a worksheet. "I did some quick calculations based on current payout rates to give us an idea of the potential reduction. Based on what you showed us, your full pension starting at age sixty-five is expected to be about $1,080 per month for your life only. If you include Linda on a joint-life basis, however, it could be as low as $850. And it could be as low as $800 if you start now rather than waiting till sixty-five."

"That's a big difference," George said, "and we sure can't afford to take that just for my life. Doesn't that mean that Linda would get no further benefit if I died early?"

"That's correct. It makes a big difference," Sarah replied.

"And while I'm asking," Mike continued, "I haven't seen any notes about long-term care insurance. Did I miss it somewhere?"

"No," Linda replied. "We hadn't given it much thought until Mom got sick."

"Most people don't until they're going through it," Sarah said. "I think you both should take a hard look at planning how you are going to cover this contingency for yourselves. As you are finding out with your mother, long-term health care can be really expensive. Mike and I see this as a big potential hole in your plan that could really cause problems down the line."

Mike interjected, "There are really four ways to plan for these expenses. One, let your kids worry about it; two, spend your assets down and rely on welfare-type plans like Medicaid; three, pass off some or all of the risk to an insurance company; or, four, assume the liability yourself and place your assets at risk. I doubt that the first two options suit you, so what about the last two—using insurance or self-insuring using your own assets?"

"Those aren't very appealing options, are they?" replied Linda. "Insurance seems really expensive, especially if we never use it. Risking all our assets could be disastrous if we both really got sick for an extended period of time. I'm not sure how to answer that question, but I know we can't ignore it. As you said, we have to have a plan."

"Let's come back to that," Sarah said. "I think it's more important at the moment to nail down potential income and see where you stand overall. Linda, have you started taking your Social Security yet? I didn't see that on any of the worksheets."

"No, I haven't. In fact, I just assumed it was best to wait until age sixty-six. I'm sixty-three now. Will that fill enough of the gap?"

"Well, it moves us closer," Sarah said. "We have some preliminary numbers for what all that would be, but we need to have you go to the Social Security website and print out a copy of your up-to-date estimates. After we get those numbers, we can fill in that blank. Based on the earnings history you told us about, I'm going to estimate that your benefit right now would be around $1,200 per month."

Mike took a sip of coffee. "OK, now let's make sure we agree on the other expenditures—what we call 'lifestyle' or 'discretionary' spending. Then we can project your overall situation. For these lifestyle expenses, you estimate that you may need an additional $2,000 per month. Is that right?"

"Yes," Linda replied. "We added up all the things we want to do—vacations and traveling, all the art classes and equipment George wants, money for the grandkids' college funds, and a little for emergencies. We also included the part of Mom's care that we're currently paying, which is about $1,000. We may have overestimated the total. But we'd rather plan for that than come up short."

"That makes sense," Sarah said. "There are a couple of issues here. First, most of your investment reserves needed to match your lifestyle expenses are in IRA and 401(k) accounts. Any money you withdraw from these will be taxed. Second, it sounds like many of the lifestyle-type expenses will be spent not on a monthly basis but as needed throughout the year. Is that correct?"

"Yes," George said. "We tried to throw everything we could think of into the bucket and divided it up monthly. Does that matter?"

"It could, but let me check some of my numbers." After doing some quick calculating, Sarah stood up at the Smart Board and said, "OK, let's see if I can summarize where we are, assuming George retires now. We have agreed that if you pay the house off, you still need around $4,400 per month for essential expenses and another $2,000 for lifestyle and emergency expenses. Is that correct?"

"Yes," Linda responded. "But that doesn't count any additional long-term care costs or other emergencies that may come up with Mom."

"Well," Sarah continued as she wrote on the board, "if we stick with the $4,400 plus $2,000 monthly number for a second, we need to figure out where the income will come from to cover these needs. Let's add up your resources. The pension will produce around $800 a month; if you both start Social Security now at age sixty-three, George's will be around $2,000, and Linda's will be $1,200. So that's only $4,000 against the $4,400. Altogether, your IRA and 401(k) accounts total $600,000. At a 4 percent withdrawal rate, those will produce about $24,000 per year, or $2,000 per month. But all that income is taxable, so the net number is closer to $1,600 per month. That brings your total income to $5,600 and more than closes your gap for essential expenses. However, you still need at least $900 per month for other expenses. If you use your $200,000 savings to cover that gap, it could be used up in a few years and would really leave you no wiggle room in the event of emergencies."

George and Linda grew still as Sarah continued. "Obviously, these are only preliminary numbers, but there are also some caveats here. First, there are large reductions for Social Security when it is taken prior to normal retirement age. Second, withdrawing 4 percent each year from your total asset base goes against the idea of matching stable or guaranteed income sources with essential expenses. Third, using IRA-type assets to this extent will create more tax liability than necessary and could shift you into a higher tax bracket."

Mike popped a graph onto the Smart Board. "Here's the bottom line, folks: Sarah and I believe that if George takes the company's early retirement package and you both fully retire, you could place yourselves at risk of running out of money. However, if you continue working until sixty-six, George, which was your original plan, your combined Social Security benefits will grow by nearly 30 percent, you can increase your savings substantially by staying in the 401(k) plan, and you will reduce the length of time that you need to fund expenses from your assets. I know that's not what you really wanted to hear, but it's better to hear the truth now, while you have choices, than in ten years, when you may not have as many options."

George looked at one line on the graph, which sagged more and more steeply as it traveled into the future, and at the alternate path that moved upward. The geometric carpet lines he had studied earlier popped into his mind as well—point by point, those lines eventually reached their destination, just with a few detours.

"Does that mean that I need to go back to work?" Linda asked.

"Not if George can continue working," Mike replied. "The ideal situation would be for George to continue working until sixty-six and to both delay taking your Social Security until full retirement age at sixty-six. That combination would really maximize your retirement dollars without drastically changing the plans you've already made or your current lifestyle."

"Let me show you what we mean," Sarah said. She went back to the Smart Board and began filling in the table. "If you wait until age sixty-six to retire, your guaranteed income sources will increase to around $5,100 per month because of increased Social Security and pension. This should easily offset your essential expenses. That extra three years could also allow you to virtually pay off the house from normal cash flow. Also, by contributing the maximum to your 401(k), you could increase your investable assets by almost $100,000. It would also give you some flexibility in how you use your IRA-type assets and your savings accounts."

MONTHLY SPENDING PLAN

Essential Monthly Expenses	$5,500
(Less Mortgage Payoff)	$(1,000)
(Less Life Insurance)	$(100)
Total Needs	$4,400
Lifestyle Expenses	+ $2,000
Total Spending Plan	$6,400

MONTHLY INCOME SOURCES

	Now	At 66
Pension Income	$800	$850
George's Social Security	$2,000	$2,700
Linda's Social Security	$1,200	$1,550
Total Stable Sources	$4,000	$5,100
401(k) & IRA After Tax	+ $1,500	+ $1,750
Total Income Sources	$5,500	$6,850

"Wow," Linda said when she saw the numbers. "That's a huge difference in only three years."

"George, do you think you have any options for work?" Mike asked.

A calm had come over George. He could see the points to his destination. "I do," he said. "I can work full time in production management at 85 percent of my current pay."

"That's definitely something," Mike said.

"But you hate management," Linda said, "and production even more!"

"That's true," he answered, "and only a couple weeks ago, I would never even have considered it a viable option. But when I look at the difference it will make in enabling us both to achieve our goals for your mother and for retirement, I see it as the best alternative. A few years of tedium so I can spend the rest of my life fulfilling my passion versus mediocrity for the rest of my days. I can't believe I'm saying this, but I think I want to postpone retirement so I can work in management. And I'm happy about it." He laughed out loud.

Linda tilted her head and looked at him with concern. Sarah, though, seemed tickled by his laughter. She chuckled herself.

"No, listen," he said. "I'm not excited by management, but I'm excited that I can see the plan laid out before me. If I do this, I know we can be confident about making the future engaging and purposeful. I now know which way to go, and I'm certain about it, even though I've never been here before. It's a solid decision."

Mike drummed his fingers on the table thoughtfully. "That might not meet all your income goals, but it could be a game changer from a retirement standpoint," he said. "We have more to discuss—first, the risk or contingency concerns, and second, the estate and legacy plan—but here's an idea: Why don't you take at least the weekend to make sure you're settled on this decision and then shoot us an e-mail? Let me and Sarah complete the rest of the income plan now that we understand all your issues."

"Plus long-term care insurance," Linda reminded them.

"Right," Mike said. "Do either of you have any potentially debilitating medical issues, such as rheumatoid arthritis or Parkinson's, that could prevent you from qualifying for insurance?"

"No, we are both healthy as horses," joked Linda.

"Good. Then, as part of our final recommendations, we will factor into the income plan a certain amount of expense for long-term care insurance and give you some options. It may be that accepting some of the risk and moving some of it to an insurance company makes the most sense. We'll just have to see what the budget looks like when we get to that point. Long-term care underwriting is a lot different from life insurance."

"I really like the idea of sharing the risk. Don't you, George?" Linda asked.

"Seems prudent," he said. "I feel certain that we're moving forward on the right path, but we'll let you know for sure on Monday."

"And we'll need a little time to pull it all together, so I'll put you down for the same time next Friday," Sarah said.

George and Linda stood up and shook hands with Mike and Sarah, thanking them. They gathered their belongings and headed home to do some final thinking about which trail they would use to descend the great retirement mountain.

16

The Plan Goes into Action

"If a man is working toward a predetermined goal and knows where he's going, that man is a success. If he's not doing that, he's a failure."

—*Earl Nightingale, motivational speaker*

George had the weekend to reconsider his decision, and at first, Linda prodded him to make sure it was what he wanted.

"I could go back to work part time," she said. "They're always looking for help."

"Thank you, Lin, but think of your job right now as being with your mother for the time we have left with her. Plus, any money we can save in her care will move us one step closer to where we want to be," George replied.

By Sunday, Linda had stopped asking about it. Instead, she came into George's workshop as he was preparing a casing for clockworks and said, "Susan is going to start meeting me at Mom's on Saturday mornings so we can cover that care shift and clean the house at the same time. Mom likes watching Miranda play anyway."

George looked up as he smoothed the wood. "I think that's a great idea."

"And I'm going to start talking with Mom about the possibility of making a move to a home now, while she can still make some friends and adjust," Linda continued. "She probably won't want to, but I can at least ask."

George dropped his sandpaper. "Linda, do I need to check you for fever?" he asked. But he was smiling.

"No," she said, laughing. "But maybe I could use a brain scan. George, I realize I've been hardheaded about Mom's situation, and I'm sorry this has put extra stress on a very stressful situation. I've been praying and thinking about this whole thing a lot, and I've really gotten a new perspective. Plus, remember how I told you about my conversation with Sarah about her in-laws' situation?"

"I do."

"She put some numbers together for me in case we needed them. They show that selling Mom's house and moving her to a continuing care retirement community makes a lot of sense for Mom and for us. The proceeds from the house will make up a significant amount of the cost difference in her care. She'll have better care, and we will gain a little financial flexibility. We may still have to pitch in a little for special things, but it won't be near the budget buster it is now."

"That's great news! I really like the way you're thinking," he said.

"But George, you were the one who finally convinced me to pursue this."

"How'd I do that? I've been trying to keep out of it and leave you alone."

"I know. But I think your attitude was really what convinced me. You knew I was struggling and gave me room even though I know it bugged the tar out of you. Then on Friday, when you agreed to take that management job you didn't like in order to make our future work, I realized that I needed to be willing to make some sacrifices, too. And really, I'm not even sure if it's a sacrifice—just a different way of looking at the situation."

"That's a really good way of putting it," George said. "Even if we make this change with your mom, I still think that taking the Southside job is the smarter choice. It gives us more freedom later, and in some weird way, it just feels like the right way to go."

Linda nodded. "So for this afternoon, why don't we drive over to this CCRC and take a tour?"

George felt like whistling a tune. But he didn't. He merely smiled at his wife and said, "It's a deal."

***

On entering the office building Monday morning, George stopped by the cafeteria for a hazelnut coffee. He still had a few minutes before his appointment with Robert. His friends Jim and Fred were once again starting the week off easy at their usual table, so George sat down to share some pleasantries.

Jim took a bite of his pastry. "This must have been from Friday's leftovers," he said. "It's hard as a rock."

"Didn't you know that's how the company is supplying the foundation for the Middleton building? Pastry by pastry," Fred said, tapping his own stiff pastry on his plate.

"How's the retirement planning going?" Jim asked George, ignoring Fred.

George took a sip of coffee. "I'm putting it off for a bit," he answered. "Going to the Southside office."

"That's too bad," Fred said. "I'm still shooting for the early gambit. Let me know if you want to sign up for that newsletter I was telling you about. It's spot on, and you get a discount any time you refer a friend."

Jim laughed. "No conflict of interest there."

"What?" Fred asked. "It's just good marketing."

"Thanks, Fred," George said. "But I've got something much more solid than gambling on those tips."

"You gonna share or what?" Fred asked.

George looked at his watch and pushed away from the table. "OK," he said, standing up and throwing away his empty cup. As he walked back past the table where his friends still sat, he winked at Jim and, smiling, said, "Here's a hot tip: find a good mountain guide."

Jim laughed again.

Fred said, "I thought you said you'd share."

George just clapped Fred on the shoulder. "Gotta go, fellas," he said.

He headed to his floor and knocked on Robert's door. It was ajar, and Robert waved him in.

"Have you figured out what date you want for your retirement lunch yet?" Robert asked. "If you jump now, you'll get the best pick."

"About that—you can put away the party plates for a while."

Robert raised an eyebrow. "Something changed?"

"As it turns out, I'm going to take that position at the Southside office after all," George admitted.

"I can't believe that was the position they chose to offer you," Robert said. "Since Worldwide decided not to keep you on here, I'm sorry you couldn't make the early retirement work."

"I appreciate that. You know, I'm not that sorry, though. Sure, I would have loved to stay on here, even part time, but this process has helped me see the future better than I'd ever imagined. I was never going to stay here forever, and now I know that what I have coming in a few years is likely bigger and better than so much of what I've done here. Who knows? I might even learn a useful something or two while I'm working at Southside."

Robert leaned back in his chair and studied George. "Seems to me I should start learning what you have these past weeks," he said. "My own time's not that far out there, after all."

"Anytime," George said. "You know where I'll be." He stood up and shook Robert's hand. "You've been a great boss, Robert. Don't be a stranger."

***

In the week that followed, Human Resources set a date for George to transfer over to Southside. The Morrises met again with Mike and Sarah, going over progress on their plan. Since they no longer had the severance lump sum to use for paying off the mortgage all at once, they decided to pay it off with Linda's Social Security over three years.

After nearly an hour had passed, Mike glanced at his watch and said, "Before we finish this meeting, I want to quickly review the last piece of our planning—the estate plan. I want to make sure we're not missing anything there. We had a chance to read through the wills that you gave us. You each have wills that mirror each other, and they are fairly recent. They state that, when one of you passes away, the other will inherit everything. In the event that you both die, then your two daughters will evenly split the estate. Is that the way you still want it?"

"Yes," replied George, "but these wills were written before we had grandchildren. Does that make any difference? I mean, should we leave money to the grandkids for college? Will there be any taxes? That really opens up a can of worms, I guess."

"It can get complicated," Mike admitted. "But let me see if I can give you a big-picture view and maybe simplify things a little. First, there are no taxes when everything goes from one spouse to the other. After you both pass away and the estate goes to your girls or to anyone else, current law allows more than $5 million per person to pass without estate taxes. So you are currently clear of any estate tax worries."

"That's good," Linda said.

"Yes," Mike said. "The only tax your heirs might have to pay is income tax on your remaining IRA and 401(k) accounts. Since these accounts have never been taxed, they will be subject to income tax when your children receive them, at your children's income tax rates. They will be taxed on the amount they withdraw from the IRA accounts as they withdraw it. So they can roll it over to an inherited IRA and stretch it out by taking the money as income, or they can withdraw it as a lump sum. That's a choice they can make at your death, and we don't need to address that now.

"But we do need to make sure the beneficiary designations on your IRA and life insurance are correct," he continued. "One of the issues many people miss is that beneficiary designations pass outside of the will. So if these are not coordinated, there can be conflicts between the beneficiary designation and the will. Also, we want to be sure not to leave money to your grandchildren outright. As minors, they cannot receive it. We can talk some more about this as we get into other planning ideas, such as college funding options and trusts."

"That's a lot of information today," George said. "I think I just reached overload."

"I agree," responded Mike. "For now, be assured that we have reviewed your basic documents, and everything is fine. We'll probably want to tweak some things, but no hurry. When we meet next week, we will have paperwork prepared to transfer some of your accounts to our management. We can handle the beneficiary designations with that paperwork."

After they agreed on a time for the next planning session, George and Linda walked to their cars. "I have to get to the office for that meeting," George said as he opened his car door.

"I know," Linda said, smiling. "But George, I feel so much better than I did a few weeks ago. I really like where we're going with this plan. I finally feel real peace of mind about our money and our overall direction."

"I do too, Lin. I'll see you this evening."

***

Two months later, George was working on a spreadsheet in his Southside office when Robert popped his head into the doorway. "Hey there, stranger. Got a minute?"

George saved the document and got up to shake Robert's hand. "Of course. What brings you to this part of town? Are you slumming it or just lost?"

"Came to see how an old friend was getting along," Robert answered.

George looked at him quizzically. "Good to see you." He pulled a chair up to his desk for Robert. "There are phones for that, too, you know."

"Yep," Robert said, sitting. "Although years in management have taught me to do some things in person."

George took his own seat again, behind his desk. "What things? Teach me—I've got to learn this management trick someday."

"Maybe not," Robert said. He looked pleased with himself.

"Do they teach management to be so mysterious? You've got that part down, apparently."

"Well, maybe not mysterious, but I have often found management to be a day or so behind schedule," Robert said.

"I give up," George replied as he leaned back. "I guess we're going to be here all day."

"Today, maybe. But next week, you could have your old office back. It's lonely."

George immediately sat up. "Just how would that work?"

Robert was flat-out grinning now. "So it turns out that, after all the dust settled, Worldwide's management finally read your report and realized that they wanted to retain the Murphy project in-house after all. Now they need someone to head it up. But what to do? They've laid off or retired all the best people in that department."

George was grinning now too. "So what did you tell them?"

"I said, 'I've maybe got the man you need, but you shoved him into management, and he may not be willing to come back.'"

"What? I'll come back," George said.

"I don't know," Robert said. "Don't be so hasty—it's only part time. It's sort of a test case for how to handle some of the other new technology projects, too, but on a limited scale. But I said to myself, 'Self, didn't George say he would have stayed even if it were part time?'"

"I did say that," George said. "But—"

"So I told management that they were fortunate this fella had stayed on with the company—and that they could maybe convince him to let go of his management position and work only part time if they re-extended his previous early retirement deal and then rehired him, guaranteeing at least half of his previous salary—maybe 75 percent, for good measure and for his trouble—until his sixty-sixth birthday."

"You said that?"

Robert nodded. "I said that. And they agreed."

"I'll take it."

Robert clapped his hands together and stood. "Excellent. Be sure that's what they offer you, then, when they call you this afternoon."

He walked to the door. "And get a move on, will you? There's some design work to be done."

George sank back into his chair as Robert closed the door behind him. It was a lot to take in. As he moved to call Linda and tell her the good news, his cell phone buzzed. It was Adam.

"How's it going, brother? Still hanging in there with the manager job?"

"Adam," George exclaimed, "you're not going to believe this!"

"Don't tell me they're talking of laying you off now," Adam said. "That makes me mad just thinking about it. Tell me where to bring the muscle, and I'll handle it for you."

George laughed. "Far from it. They're going to give me my old job back—but better. I'll get retirement benefits plus part-time work on the project I was most invested in."

"And that project is something you really want to do?"

"Yeah, I'll say! It's an experimental venture to develop a portable water desalination process. It's exactly the kind of technology I want to be able to take to areas all over the world that have limited access to clean water. It could change the lives of thousands of people if I can get it developed and usable. The interesting thing is that I learned how to advocate with the big boys for it by going through the planning process that Linda and I followed for retirement. It taught me how to think strategically, and this let us put together a proposal that the new company liked, even though the project didn't fit into their main line of business. Who knew I could be a promoter like my big brother?"

"I always knew there was a salesman in there somewhere," Adam said. "So let me get this straight—you are going to continue to work part time for the next few years on your pet project, get paid to follow your dream, and still have time to do other stuff?"

George felt a little light-headed, even giddy. "Can you believe it? Just think. If I had never figured out my retirement dreams, I

"I really want to make the rest of my years count for something. I don't want to be that bitter old retired guy who watches the news all day, complains to anyone who will listen, and tries to relive his past glories."

wouldn't have taken this management job, which made me available for this opportunity, and I wouldn't have known this opportunity would give me the best of both worlds: part-time work in something I still enjoy, as well as an opportunity that can fuel a future full of possibilities"

"I think I'm a little jealous," Adam replied.

"You know, even if this job hadn't turned up, Linda and I still had a map down the retirement mountain to our promised land—a map that showed us how to descend without wearing out either our money or our significance along the way. I'd be happy to share some of the information and worksheets we used to get here."

Adam stayed quiet for a moment. Then he said, "I think I'd like that. I see what you're doing, and I've realized I really want to make the rest of my years count for something. I don't want to be that bitter old retired guy who watches the news all day, complains to anyone who will listen, and tries to relive his past glories." He cleared his throat. "Just one thing . . ."

"What's that?"

"Would you also be willing to give me a little coaching with all these magical worksheets you've talked about? You've discovered a new excitement about living a meaningful life. And that's what I want, too."

"I will, and I'll do you one better than that—I'll give you your own advice. It's not too late for you to ask for help from a financial planner. I can give you Mike's number, if you want."

"Now that I've seen what he's done for you, I think I'll take it."

***

The rest of the week flew by in a whirlwind of meetings regarding the new job offer and bringing George's replacement at the Southside position up to speed. George and Linda sent the news over to Mike and Sarah, who adjusted their financial plan once again, reworked their investments to match their new situation, and walked them through some important details, such as negotiating favorable health-insurance coverage until George turned sixty-five, when he would be covered by Medicare.

That weekend their family came to Sunday dinner. As Linda dished out food, their grown children, the children's spouses, and George's brother and his family gathered around the table. Grandchildren and grandnieces and nephews spilled out onto the sunporch. Sliding a portion of lasagna onto Adam's wife's plate, Linda told her, "I've begun exploring other housing options for Mom, and after visiting a few places, she doesn't seem to be so resistant. It's really made a difference in our outlook. I'm so glad one of our financial planners shared her personal experience with me. It was like we—or I—were stuck holding on to something that I needed to let go of."

George smiled at the changes that had occurred in a few short months because they had taken the time to step back and assess what was most important to them. As the two ladies sat down, George looked over the blessings all around him. He bowed his head to say grace, but first, he gave a private little prayer of thanks, whispering to himself, "Then you will know which way to go, since you have never been this way before."

Notes

1. Pew Research Center, *Growing Old in America: Expectations vs. Reality*, June 29, 2009, www.pewsocialtrends.org/2009 /06/29/growing-old-in-america-expectations-vs-reality.

2. Bob Buford, *Halftime: Moving from Success to Significance* (Grand Rapids, MI: Zondervan, 2008).

3. William Shakespeare, *The Tempest*, ed. Martin Butler (Boston: Penguin, 2007), act 2, scene 1, line 252.

4. Phil. 3:13–14a (NIV).

5. Josh. 3:4 (NIV).

6. Marcus Buckingham and Donald Clifton, *Now, Discover Your Strengths* (New York: The Free Press, 2001), 6.

7. Ibid., 7.

8. Ibid., 25–26.

9. "Gallup Strengths Center," Gallup, Inc., accessed April 5, 2016, www.gallupstrengthscenter.com/Home/en-US/About.

10. Chip Ingram, *Good to Great in God's Eyes: 10 Practices Great Christians Have in Common* (Grand Rapids, MI: Baker, 2009), 146.

11. Charles Duhigg, *The Power of Habit: Why We Do What We Do in Life and Business* (New York: Random House, 2012), 23.

12. Ben D. Gardner, "Busting the 21 Days Habit Formation Myth," *Health Chatter: The Health Behavior Research Centre Blog*, June

29, 2012, blogs.ucl.ac.uk/hbrc/2012/06/29/busting-the-21-days-habit-formation-myth.

13. Chip Ingram, *Good to Great in God's Eyes: 10 Practices Great Christians Have in Common,* (Grand Rapids, MI: Baker, 2009), 81.

14. Dalbar, Inc., *2015 Quantitative Analysis of Investor Behavior,* 2015, www.dalbar.com.

15. Ibid.

16. Gary P. Brinson, L. Randolph Hood, and Gilbert. L. Beebower, "Determinants of Portfolio Performance," *Financial Analysts Journal* 42, no. 4 (July–August 1986).

17. "A Guide to Asset Allocation," *2014 Franklin Templeton Investments* (San Mateo, CA: Franklin Templeton Investments, 2014): 4.

18. William F. Sharpe, "Likely Gains from Market Timing," *Financial Analysts Journal* 31, no. 2 (March–April 1975): 60-69, www.jstor.org/stable/4477805.

19. H. Nejat Seyhun and Wesley G. McCain, *Stock Market Extremes and Portfolio Performance 1926–2004: A study commissioned by Towneley Capital Management and conducted by Professor H. Nejat Seyhun, University of Michigan* (Laguna Hills, CA: Towneley Capital Management, Inc., 2005), 10. Cited with permission of Towneley Capital Management, Inc. For complete text of the study, see www.Towneley.com.

20. These points measure the actual historical return and risk characteristics of stocks as measured by the S&P 500® Index and of bonds as measured by Barclay's US Aggregate Bond Index.

For over thirty-five years, Andy Raub has helped countless individuals plan their financial futures and manage their investments. He founded Raub Capital Management, a top advisory firm, to focus on retirement planning. An early baby boomer, he understands the fears most retirees face, and he has created the Encore Curve program to help retirees reset their life goals and reorganize their money so they can live with renewed purpose. Andy is known as America's Encore Coach and is a sought-after speaker on personal finance and life-planning topics, as well as a popular Bible teacher. He holds a BS in psychology and an MBA in finance from the University of North Texas and has attended Dallas Theological Seminary. Andy is also an elder in his church and has served on numerous nonprofit boards. He lives in Dallas with his wife, Jean, and is called Dad by their two grown daughters and Dandy by four teenage grandchildren.